CHRISTIANITY
WITHOUT INSANITY

FOR OPTIMAL
MENTAL/EMOTIONAL/PHYSICAL HEALTH

ChristianityWithoutInsanity.com

Boyd C. Purcell, Ph.D.
Author of *Spiritual Terrorism*
HealingSpiritualTerrorism.com

Bible Study/
Discussion
Questions at
End of Each
Chapter

Christianity Without Insanity
Boyd C. Purcell, Ph.D.

www.ChristianityWithoutInsanity.com

International Standard Book Number
ISBN—13: 978-1478322382

Printed in The United States of America

CreateSpace
Charleston, South Carolina

DEDICATION

This book is dedicated to my five adorable, beautiful, curious, intelligent, loving, wonderful, and life/fun-loving grandchildren. May they grow up in a tolerant, peaceful world where all forms of bigotry, bullying, discrimination, violence, war, and child abuse—physical, mental, emotional, sexual, and spiritual—have been abolished! Universal understanding of universal salvation will herald The Gospel—Good News—of this glorious future!

Contents

Introduction

My book, *Spiritual Terrorism: Spiritual Abuse from the Womb to the Tomb,* was published in April of 2008. Since then I have been receiving emails from across the country and from around the world, informing me of the help people have been receiving from reading my book. Victims of spiritual terrorism have been finding peace with God, tranquility of mind, healing for damaged emotions, and joy of living.[1] There are 83 reviews of *Spiritual Terrorism* on Amazon.com, and 75 are 5-stars [the highest] rated.

I did not write *Spiritual Terrorism* to be controversial, inflammatory, or sensational but to be descriptive. In this book, *Christianity Without Insanity*, it is my intention to be helpful to as many victims of spiritual insanity as possible, speaking the truth in love. Christianity is a wonderful religion, and, by way of personal self-disclosure, I am a Trinitarian Christian. I agree with the late-great, Christian writer George MacDonald who believed that the Christian faith is so wonderful, lofty, and liberating that it is susceptible to being misunderstood and perverted. That explains a great deal about why there is so much anxiety, fear, and terror in the Christian faith today. It thus has been seriously perverted, misunderstood, and used to terrorize many people by Christian officials who are well intentioned but ill informed.

There are, of course, some Christian Church officials who are ill intentioned and well informed. That was the case in church history, which is the reason why the truth of **Christian Universalism (CU)** was perverted to the doctrine of eternal damnation for the vast majority of the human race and salvation for relatively few. I documented the facts as to how, when, and why it happened, in *Spiritual Terrorism*. My purpose in *Christianity Without Insanity* is to build on that information, give updated material, and real-life examples of people who have been healed of the health-destroying effects of spiritual terrorism, in this book, I identify as "spiritual insanity!" In *Spiritual Terrorism,* my goal was to be definitive; thus, it is a book of almost 500 pages. My goal in this book is to be concise with equal clarity.

Eternal "damnationists" insist that eternal torment is the "traditional doctrine" of hell. I contend that CU is the original truth taught by our Lord Jesus Christ. He castigated the Pharisees for worshiping God with their lips, but not with their hearts, and teaching for doctrine the commandments of men (Mt. 15:7-9). Hell fear mongers are modern-day Pharisees. Paul warned believers to turn away from those who have a form of Godliness but deny the power thereof (II Tim. 3:5). Those preaching eternal torture in hell are denying the power, love, and will of God to save all people!

This book would be ideal to be used as a Sunday school quarterly or adult Bible study, since there are 12 chapters with discussion questions at the end of each one. In a 13-week quarter, the first week could be devoted to studying and discussing the oxymorons and the acrostic "INSANITY," at the beginning of chapter one, and then one chapter per week for the rest of the quarter. There is easily enough material to be used for two consecutive quarters. This book is intended primarily for lay adults and young people, but clergy may well learn from it. Contact information is included, and I welcome comments or questions. There is a great deal of information which is free on my websites: HealingSpiritualTerrorism.com; ChristianityWithoutInsanity.com.

Is the beautiful picture of the sun over water, on the cover of this book, a sunrise or sunset? Illustratively, it is actually both. It is a sunset on the insanely false doctrine of eternal torture in hell fire. It is a sunrise on the glorious truth of CU! I believe we are in the beginning of a new Reformation, which is transforming the whole Christian Church—Anglican, Eastern Orthodox, Protestant, Roman Catholic—and will, combined, far surpass the magnitude of the split of the Orthodox Church in 1054, the Protestant Reformation in 1517, and the Anglican Schism in 1534 in regard to the impact on Christianity and the world! This is the reverse process of purifying and reuniting the Christian Church into the unity for which Jesus prayed in His high-priestly prayer we would all be one just as He and our heavenly Father are One (John 17). What invention of movable-type printing, in 1440, did making possible the Reformation of salvation by grace, the Internet will do for this new **Reformation of Salvation by Grace of ALL**!

Chapter 1
Christianity With Insanity

The "C" in the acrostic "CHRISTIANITY" represents "Christianity With Insanity." Christianity with insanity is spiritually life taking, enslaving, controlling, and deforming. Christianity without insanity is spiritually life giving, freeing, empowering, and transforming!

An acrostic—using each letter in a word to represent a particular point—is an excellent memory device and teaching tool. In order, therefore, to clearly understand the spiritual insanity in fear-based, so-called Orthodox Christianity, I have created two acrostics using the words, "Insanity" [next page] and "Christianity" [as seen in the "Contents," each letter forming chapters 1-12].

The word "oxymoron" comes from two Greek words, "oxus," meaning sharp or keen, and "moras," meaning dull or foolish [the origin of moron jokes]. Therefore, the word "oxymoron" is itself an oxymoron, since it expresses two inherently contradictory things. Looking at the big picture of the Christian faith, the most obvious thing Christianity must be without to be love based rather than fear based is oxymorons. Here is my list of the top ten:

The Top Ten Oxymorons of Fear-Based Christianity

10. God's perfectly proportional justice and eternal hell
9. God's desire that none perish and almost all perish
8. God's sovereignty overruled by human free will
7. God's omniscience and inability to change free will
6. God's omnipotence and impotence to save all persons
5. God's omnipresence and eternal separation from God
4. God's amazing grace and eternal punishment in hell
3. God's unconditional love and eternal torment in hell
2. God's everlasting love and eternal damnation in hell
1. God's infinite mercy and eternal torture in hell

This is the spiritually insane "oxymoronic gospel" that Biblical literalists believe! Tragically, this creates spiritual morons who teach that the "unelect" who die in infancy will be condemned to hell eternally, and unbaptized infants will be forever banished from God's presence. **Spiritual insanity is the unbiblical-illogical belief that God, <u>who is love</u>, will torture all non-Christians and the "wrong kind of Christians" in the fire of hell forever!**

Thus, oxymorons must be eliminated from Christianity in order to cure spiritual insanity, not cause it. Like a skilled surgeon cutting out a cancerous tumor from a patient's body, spiritual insanity is what The Great Physician is in the process of excising from the Body of Christ—His Church. To visualize this inherent insanity, I have developed the acrostic "I-N-S-A-N-I-T-Y."

The Insanity in So-Called Orthodox Christianity

I-nsane hypocrisy of God torturing His enemies in hell fire for-ever, thus, violating His own law of proportionality to the nth degree (Ex.21:23-25) and Christ's command to forgive, do good for, and even love one's enemies (Mt. 5:38-44; 18:21, 22)

N-onsense of God's everlasting love not lasting (Jer. 31:3)

S-avior of the world not saving the world (John 1:29; 4:42)

A-tonement for all not atoning for all (Rom. 5:10-21)

N-ever-failing love [agape] of God failing (I Cor. 13:8)

I-nfinite mercy [KJV] of God not enduring forever (Ps. 136)

T-hwarting God's plan of salvation [impossible] (Job 42:2 NIV)

Y-ou are saved by grace through faith (Eph. 2:8, 9), **but** must keep all of God's commandments, obey all church rules, and believe, worship, and live "right," and tithe
<u>CU is the original Orthodox faith founded by Jesus, God incarnate!</u>

Horrific Case of Spiritual Insanity

There is no better example of spiritual insanity than the horrific case of Andrea Yates who killed all five of her young children in Houston, Texas, June 20, 2001. God, according to Biblical literalists, does not just command the execution of children, who will not obey their parents, (Deut. 21), God will do far worse—judge, condemn, and throw them into literal hell fire eternally!

Preachers, who are literalists and legalists, often quote Jesus, per the KJV, **"Be ye therefore perfect, even as your Father in heaven is perfect"** (Mt. 5:48). Children, who have reached the "age of accountability," as well as adults, must accept Christ and live "right"—be spiritually perfect! Even if one has accepted Christ, dying suddenly without having confessed every sin, means being condemned to the fire of hell, on Judgment Day, where there will be eternal weeping and gnashing of teeth (Mt. 13:40-42).

Catholics believe in purgatory where they will go to suffer for venial sins [mortal sins are forever] and then go on to heaven. But with Protestants, who do not believe in purgatory, it is all or nothing—heaven or eternal hell! This crazy theology appears to be what pushed AndreaYates over the edge to killing all her children: Noah (7), John (5), Paul (3), Luke (2), and Mary (6 months)!

Yates had been diagnosed with post-partum depression and psychosis and was treated with strong antipsychotic medications in psychiatric facilities until her medical-insurance coverage was exhausted. She was then discharged. Under Texas' definition of insanity, Andrea was declared to be legally sane. Millions of women, who give birth, suffer from post-partum depression and, some, psychosis. Some also have various mental illnesses, but they do not kill their children.

With experience as a psychotherapist in a psychiatric hospital, my mind naturally asks, "What was it about Yates' situation which caused her to murder her five children?" Even if she were not legally insane, Yates was certainly spiritually insane due to the insane religious teaching she had been receiving for years under the "ministry" of a Christian evangelist, Michael Woroniecki. He grew up in Roman Catholicism and became a Protestant and then developed his brand of literalistic, hell-fire Christianity. Nothing I am saying is to deny individual responsibility; it is only to explain the apparently inexplicable and put it in context.

Andrea and Rusty Yates met at Auburn University, got married, and moved to Houston where she gave birth to five children in about ten years. Five young children would put a lot of stress on any mother, but the mother would get some relief if the older children went daily to preschool, kindergarten, and/or elementary school. But Andrea, trying to be the super mom and spiritual mom, was home schooling which is what her religious instruction said she was supposed to do. Having several young children close in age can be exhausting for a mother, not just to give birth but to care for them 24 hours a day seven days a week.

Understandably, Andrea had been suffering from depression. Her depression worsened and she twice attempted suicide because she thought Satan was in her and that her children would be destroyed and go to hell because she was a bad mom. She reasoned that if she could kill herself, God might have mercy on her children. When she was unsuccessful in taking her life, the thoughts came into her head that she needed to do the best thing for her children, before they were corrupted by the evil world, and kill them so they could go on to heaven.

I know this sounds crazy, because it is crazy, but, based on her insanely false religious brainwashing, **in context,** it makes sense. She apparently reasoned thusly: Why would any loving parents stand by and let their children almost certainly go to hell, to be tortured forever, when they could send them on to heaven?

I heard only one mention of the religious aspect on the media coverage, but, as soon as I heard it, I thought that it was probably a major factor in the horrible tragedy that took place when Andrea murdered all of her children. At the trial, the prosecutors asked for a guilty verdict and the death sentence. The jury found her guilty but gave her life in prison. After the trial, there was a documentary on TV which did a good job of exposing the religious insanity. There is a lot of information on various websites from which I have been able to put together the pieces of the religious puzzle. There are more pieces to the puzzle of this horrible and unnecessary tragedy which you can read in *Spiritual Terrorism*, but here the focus is on brevity.

After Yates killed her children, a psychiatrist came to see her in jail and asked her about what she understood her religious teachings to mean about her as a mother. She gave this response: **"The way I was raising them they could never be saved. They were doomed to perish in the fires of hell."** Yates could simply be written off as a horrible person whom the state should execute and God should send to hell. Some people would probably agree that this is her due punishment. But what she believed about eternal hell fire is essentially what many Christian Churches teach about children and eternal damnation.

No, I am not saying that Christian Churches teach parents that they should kill their children; they certainly do not. What they do teach about eternal punishment in hell fire is frightening to many normal people and is enough to give the final push to drive some already emotionally unstable persons over the edge to spiritual, if not mental insanity. They also teach God is going to do far worse to children who do not accept Christ and please God.

She killed her children in order to send them to heaven, but God will judge, condemn, and torture children who do not please Him in hell fire forever! *If the churches which teach it are right,* some children, even infants, will suffer punishment or banishment eternally through no fault of their own—God did not "elect" them for salvation, or their parents failed to have them baptized. All such teaching is theological nonsense, spiritual terrorism, and spiritual insanity! Spiritual terrorism causes spiritual insanity. The spiritually insane may commit insane acts of terrorism.

John Gerstner, in 1990, wrote the book, *Repent or Perish*[1] which was endorsed by John White, the then President of the National Association of Evangelicals. The NAE represents 30 million conservative Christians in the USA. In Gerstner's warped theology, Yates' children are burning in hell, now and forever, because they were not old enough to know that they needed to be born again and, therefore, could not make the decision to accept Christ. Yates, apparently, believed what most Fundamentalists and Evangelicals believe that children who die before reaching "the age of accountability" (usually age 12) will go to heaven.

No, I have never heard even one preacher preach that parents should kill their children before the age of accountability in order to make sure that they go to heaven. But what they do preach about eternal damnation in literal hell fire, after the age of accountability, may cause some unstable persons, such as Andrea, to do that in order to save their children.

Kill them to save them? Of course, it is crazy thinking; that is why it is spiritual insanity!

In spite of churches preaching the doctrine of eternal damnation in hell, virtually all Christian parents are very devoted to protecting, not harming, their children. I have counseled with loving mothers who were extremely fearful that their children might grow up and not accept Christ and be damned to hell fire forever. They have said that believing in Christian Universalism (CU) would make it so much easier to trust their children to God!

For many years the late John Gerstner was a member of the mainline Presbyterian Church in the United States of America (PCUSA) until it, apparently, became too "liberal" for him. The PCUSA passed a bylaw which stated, "We believe that all dying in infancy are included in the election of grace, and are regenerated and saved by Christ through the Spirit, who works when and where and how he pleases."[2] In 1990 Gerstner switched his membership to the small but conservative Presbyterian Church in America (PCA). He died in 1996.

Frightened by a survey finding that Evangelical Christians, including one third of all college and seminary students, have rejected the doctrine of eternal punishment, the President of the National Association of Evangelicals (NAE), in 1990, apparently encouraged Gerstner to write a book in defense of this doctrine. The result was the publication of, *Repent or Perish.* If this book only represented the extreme views of Gerstner, I would not even bother quoting any of his theological statements, but **the NAE represents 30 million Evangelical Christians in 45 thousand churches in America.** Churches teaching such theology are centers of spiritual abuse causing spiritual insanity.

President White wrote the foreword to Gerstner's book in which he highly praised him for such a fine work. He concluded, "The Evangelical community needs the clarity, logic, and forthrightness that have always been the style of John Gerstner. Dr. Gerstner, we are again indebted to you and we say—'thank you.'" White claims that this book expresses Evangelical theology. Gerstner contends that it is the "right" interpretation for all "true" Christians.

Exactly what is it for which Evangelical Christians are supposed to be thankful and indebted to Gerstner? Is this quote wise counsel or spiritual insanity? Readers, you decide:

> Why, then, do almost all seem to oppose frightening children with hell? The answer is obvious: they wrongly fancy that children are not in danger of hell. There are three imagined reasons for supposing that children are in no danger of hell. Some think children are innocent of sin and guilt. Some admit that they are not innocent, but are saved from sin by being born again in infant baptism. Some fancy that though little sinners, not regenerated in baptism, children are, nonetheless, safe in the covenant of grace. Infants are not innocent, but born in guilt and sin. So until children are born again, they are in imminent peril of

eternal damnation and should be made aware of it as soon as possible.[3]

Calvinists, like Gerstner, certainly believe that unborn babies are conceived in guilt and sin! Based on this theological point-of-view, "non-elect" fetuses miscarried or babies still born will be condemned to eternal hell fire even though they never breathed a breath of air, never saw the light of day, and never committed even one sin! **Forget theology, just plain common sense and basic logic says that this is a case of horrific spiritual insanity!** Lay readers with good common sense may well see this as nonsensical and even idiotic. **Such theology defames the name of God, insults the love of God, and negates the grace of God!**

It also causes spiritual insanity! No wonder one third of all Evangelical college and seminary students have rejected the doctrine of eternal punishment! But what about the two thirds who still believe it? What will happen to expectant mothers who read Gerstner's book and take it seriously? And what about those who sit in the pews of those 45 thousand churches represented by the NAE and hear this kind of hell-fire preaching week after week and month after month? Their stress level will be elevated, worsening their natural maternal fears that "something might happen" to their babies. This will, at the same time, negatively affect the development of babies in the womb due to such stress.

A Distinctive of Western Christianity

This senseless doctrine that babies who have not been baptized will go to hell or "at best" be forever barred from beholding the face of God is a distinctive of Western Christianity—Catholicism and Calvinistic Protestantism. Augustine's view of original sin has had a profoundly negative impact on Christianity in the West [Western Europe and North and South America]. Bishop Timothy Ware of the Eastern Orthodox Church makes this point. "And Orthodox have never held (as Augustine and many others in the West have done) that unbaptized babies, because of being tainted with original guilt, are consigned by the just God to the everlasting flames of hell. The Orthodox picture of fallen humanity is far less somber than the Augustinian or Calvinist view."[4] To its credit, in addition to water baptism, the Catholic Church teaches baptism by fire/blood [martyrdom] and desire [for those who would have believed if they had heard the Gospel]; would this not save infants?

Update on Andrea Yates

On March 27, 2012, various media reported that Yates might be released by the court from the mental institution, where she has been confined, since winning her guilty-verdict appeal, to be able to attend Sunday services at a church in the Houston area. It has been over ten years since she murdered her children. Andrea is now 47 and is not going to be having more children, so she is no threat to kill children she might have. She will be no threat to other people's children, since she would feel no responsibility for them. George Parnham, her attorney, said that the teachings of the church she wants to attend are 180 degrees different than the hell-fire teachings of the evangelist which caused her to kill her children.

According to Parnham, Yates just wants God to be a positive factor in her life. Parnham did not say which church had agreed to accept her. The type of church, in the Houston area, which has teachings opposite of what Yates had been taught is the Lakewood Church, pastored by Rev. Joel Osteen. In *Spiritual Terrorism*, I mentioned it as an example of a non-spiritually abusive church that has grown, according to Church Growth Today, to be the largest church in the USA. Each Sunday 38,000 people attend services. He does not preach the false doctrine of eternal punishment in hell fire. Osteen's spiritually inspiring sermons are built on love-based Christianity, practical psychology, and positive thinking.

Another Case of Murder

It is not just the fear of children going to hell which may cause spiritually insane people to commit murder. Religiously insane people, including Christians, may murder in the name of God due to fear of divine wrath in this life or even eternal hell if they don't.

How does a man, honorably discharged from the military service of The United States, wanting to find Biblical answers to life's problems, end up sentenced to life in prison for multiple murders? The case of Ronald Luff illustrates this spiritual insanity.

Criminal MindScape, on MSNBC, is a special series for the purpose of trying to understand the mind of criminals who have committed felonies, especially murder. In the interview with Ron Luff, he stated that he had joined a Bible-study group, in Kirtland, Ohio, just to try to find answers to some of life's perplexing problems. This was a splinter group from the Church of Jesus Christ of Latter Day Saints. The leader was Jeffrey Lundgren.

To make a long story short, Lundgren taught that Jesus' Second Coming was being prevented by sin in the group. He taught that they needed to do everything possible to be pure and holy so Christ could come again for His Second Advent and set everything right with the world. As time went on, Lundgren fixated on one family in the group, Dennis Avery (49), and his wife, Cheryl (46), and daughters Trina (17), Rebecca (15), and Karen (7). Lundgren convinced the group that this family, due to the sin of withholding money from the group, had to be eliminated. On April 17, 1989, Luff distracted this family while the rest of the group dug a large pit in a barn and, one-by-one, led each one into the barn where Lundgren shot and killed them. The group shoveled dirt over them and then went to the house and held a prayer meeting!

This horrible crime was later discovered, and the members of this group were arrested, indicted, and tried for murder. Some members cooperated and testified against Lundgren and received lighter sentences with the possibility of parole. Lundgren was convicted of capital murder and was executed by the state of Ohio on October 24, 2006. Luff was convicted of murder and sentenced to 170 years in prison which means no possibility of parole. It was Luff, convicted by his conscience, who had gone to the police to report the murders. Thus, he was spared the death sentence. In the interview with "Criminal MindScape," Luff seemed like a normal, sensible, and reasonable person who was truly sorry for his crimes.

He realized way too late not to take everything in *the Bible* literally and act on erroneous conclusions.

Any sane person will logically ask, "How could anyone get the idea of committing murder from reading and studying *the Bible*?" There are many stories of violence, war, murder, and mayhem in *The Torah,* Christians know as *The Old Testament.* Such a story is that of Achan in the seventh chapter of the Book of Joshua. Due to the sin of Achan, causing the Israelites to lose a battle, according to the text, they stoned Achan and his whole family to death. This, they believed, removed sin from their midst! The message is to get rid of all sin at all cost! Based on this Biblical story, there is an old saying in the form of a question, in regard to a group, "Is there an 'Achan' [sin] in the camp?" [If you doubt this, Google this term.] There is an individual application, "Is there an 'Achan' in your life?"

Murder in the Name of God

George Tiller was a medical doctor who provided health care for women which included the practice of abortion. Scott Roeder (51) was an Evangelical Christian who was adamantly opposed to abortion for any reason, since he believed it is the taking of human life. Dr. Tiller was a Lutheran who attended church regularly, but he held a different Christian worldview than did Roeder. Roeder stalked Tiller for two years, and then on May 31, 2009, walked into the Lutheran Church on Sunday morning, in Wichita, Kansas, and gunned down Dr. Tiller in cold blood—taking human life Roeder vehemently opposed.

The Bible instructs Christians not to overcome evil with evil but to overcome evil with good (Rom. 12:21). Apparently, Roeder did not read his Bible well enough to understand this admonition of the Apostle Paul or just chose to ignore it. Roeder was hoping to put the issue of abortion on trial, but that did not happen. On January 9, 2010, after deliberating for just 37 minutes, a jury found Roeder guilty of first-degree murder. He is facing life in prison.

David Koresh, "the final prophet," led his followers of 70 to their deaths, including 21 children, at the Branch Dividian Compound in 1993 in Waco, Texas. Eric Rudolph, a Fundamental Christian, bombed an abortion center in Atlanta, Georgia, during the Summer Olympics in 1996. He committed other bombings, killing five people and wounding a total of at least 150. He is now serving a life sentence for his spiritually insane murders in God's name. Rev. Paul Hill, a Presbyterian Minister, who assassinated an abortion doctor, was executed by the state of Florida in 2003. Timothy McVeigh was a Catholic who, on April 19, 1995, bombed the Murrah Federal Building in Oklahoma City killing 168 and wounding over 500 innocent men, women, and children in his vendetta against what he perceived to be big-bad, gone-wrong government. His murders were far worse than that for which he had blamed the government, loss of lives at Waco and Ruby Ridge.

McVeigh was executed by the Federal Government on June 11, 2001. His last request was to see a Catholic priest. The Catholic Church teaches that priests have the authority to forgive sins. If this is true and McVeigh confessed his sins of murder, and the priest forgave him, then McVeigh will be in heaven via purgatory. But his victims, if they were non-Christians or Christians who had committed even one unconfessed sin, before suddenly being murdered, will be condemned by God to hell forever. This is what Christians who believe in the insanely false doctrine of eternal torment in hell fire generally believe about God!

Another terrible case of spiritual insanity was that of the Rev. Jim Jones who left the USA with his followers to establish a communal-living colony at Jonestown [named for himself], in Guyana, South America. In 1978, at Jonestown, he led 909 people— including 200 children—in a mass suicide to get away from the sinful evil world. That was mass spiritual insanity!

In all of these examples not one murderer was declared to be legally insane. All of these cases are examples of spiritual insanity!

18

A Death Unintentional But Foreseeable

All of this murder and mayhem in the name of God is spiritual insanity. While spiritual insanity may not lead to murder, it has, at times, led to the deaths of innocent people. Such was the case of James from the state of Oregon. After reading my book, *Spiritual Terrorism,* James contacted me to share his profoundly tragic story. He related that his mother was in her late thirties and had some health problems when she was engaged to his father. She was a devout Catholic; his father was also Catholic but not devout.

Before getting married, James' mother went to her doctor to have a physical examination. Based on the exam and her medical history, her physician advised her not to get pregnant because, based on his best medical opinion, she had a high probability of having toxemia (blood poisoning) causing complications that could result in the loss of her baby and/or her own life.

The Roman Catholic Church taught then [70 years ago] and still teaches today that the only acceptable means of birth control are abstinence or rhythm, based on a woman's menstrual cycle. All other means of birth control are labeled by the Catholic Church as "artificial," and it is a mortal sin to use "artificial" means of birth control. Mortal sins carry the penalty of eternal damnation in hell fire! Readers, have you heard what they call couples who practice only rhythm as a means of birth control? Parents!

Birth-control pills had not yet been developed, but, as a devout Catholic, she could not use an IUD or other "artificial" means of birth control without putting her soul in danger of eternal punishment in hell fire. She went to her priest to explain her situation and ask his advice. After hearing the explanation of her circumstances, the priest told her to obey God rather than man. And what, per the priest, did God want her to do? As God told Adam and Eve, "Be fruitful and multiply." To give this priestly counsel in the light of this woman's age, health condition, her doctor's recommendation, and the fact the world was already well populated, is another very glaring case of spiritual insanity.

19

"Page two" of James' and his mother's story: She did get married, she did not use "artificial" means of birth control, she did get pregnant, she did have complications, she did die, and James almost died. James shared the story his father had told him about his mother and the circumstances of her death as he was growing up. James felt very guilty about his mother dying as she gave birth to him. His father was bitter and went to church only on Christmas and Easter. James heard in church about God, Christ, heaven, purgatory, and eternal hell fire.

At about 12 years of age James stated that he had heard enough and decided that he wanted nothing more to do with church, so he turned off and dropped out for many years. Later in life he began to explore his spirituality. In the course of his spiritual journey, he discovered my book, read it, and the message of CU made perfect sense to him, he stated. He liked my book so well that he wrote a five-star review of it and posted it on Amazon.com. James is now a lay minister in the Unity Church which does not teach the false doctrine of eternal hell fire.

The Holy Bible says not one word about birth control. The only thing that even comes remotely close to saying something about this subject, which is a major issue in the Catholic Church, is the story of Onan (Gen. 38:6-11).

According to Jewish custom, the eldest son inherited the family farm. If he died without having a son, a younger brother was to marry his widow. If this marriage produced a son, he would have become his deceased brother's heir, not the younger brother. Therefore, Onan, the younger brother did not want to disinherit himself, so he practiced withdrawal to prevent conception, and per the text, God struck him dead.

Is this literally true or did Onan simply have a heart attack or stroke? Ancient peoples thought God caused everything they did not understand. Since they did not understand heart attacks and strokes, might they have drawn an erroneous conclusion that God had taken his life for refusing to provide an heir for his brother?

Psychic Determinism

There is a term for connecting, in one's mind, two unrelated events happening closely in time—"psychic determinism." This is the basis of all superstition and a lot of religion. For example, the late Rev. Dr. Jerry Falwell and others preached that Hurricane Katrina was due to God's judgment on America for the sins of abortion and homosexuality. Obviously, few cases of spiritual insanity result in murder or even unintentional deaths. But spiritual insanity may well lead to chronic and/or acute stress, panic attacks, depression, delusions, psychiatric care (including hospitalization), etc. This we will see in the next chapter, "Holistic Health."

Discussion Questions

1. Does it make sense that fear-based Christianity causes spiritual insanity? What about psychic determinism?
2. Some Christians who believe all children go to heaven, who die before "the age of accountability," have called abortion doctors the most effective "soul savers" in the world. What do you think?
3. Is it not spiritually insane to fight against abortion because it is taking "innocent" human life but, teach that the same babies, if "unelect," will be forever condemned to hell?
4. What about babies who die unbaptized? Would it be fair for God to forever banish them from His presence due to parental failure? Is this possible per Psalm 139:7, 8?
5. What do you think about baptism by water, fire, or desire?
6. According to Job, no plan of God can be thwarted (42:2). How could God's plan to save all (I Tim. 2:4) be defeated?
7. Have you heard the term, "An Achan"? How can people be manipulated into doing horrible things by literally applying O.T. stories to today?
8. In your opinion, are birth control measures, to prevent conception, against God's will? Why or why not? How do you interpret the story of Onan? Is God's command to Adam and Eve to be "fruitful" an obligation for all today?

Chapter 2
Holistic Health

The "H" in the acrostic "CHRISTIANITY" represents "Holistic Health," the medical scientific truth that the person as a whole, not separate parts, optimizes mental/emotional/physical well-being. Please notice the slash between the aspects of human well-being, rather than commas, because these parts cannot be separated. Holistic health, by definition, is integral to and inseparable from the whole person. Healthy spirituality is inherent in holistic health, but, to be clear in the formulation of this logical truth, spirituality is first: spiritual/mental/emotional/physical health.

I have taught psychopathology in the Counseling Department at Marshall University Graduate College to students earning their Master Degree. Psychopathology holds that there is an integral and inseparable relationship between mind and body. What affects the mind affects the body and what affects the body affects the mind—the whole person. Emotionally, the human nervous system cannot distinguish between what is true and what is believed to be true and is vividly imagined to have happened or might happen. Any such situation can cause an extreme nervous reaction.

Dr. Lewis Whaley, an oncologist, endorsed my book, *Spiritual Terrorism*, with this statement. "As a physician, I can validate Dr. Purcell's understanding of psychopathology. The anxiety which religion, or any other factor, generates has the potential to depress the human immune system, affect every organ, and impair bodily functions."

Rational Emotive Therapy (RET) is based on the principle that feelings are caused by thoughts. If people want to know why they are feeling a certain way, they need to ask themselves what they have been thinking. Changing negative to positive thoughts will change negative feelings to positive ones. According to RET, therefore, spiritual beliefs/practices impact mental thinking which cause feelings that have a profound effect, for good or bad, on one's physical health. The case of Jay is very illustrative.

Healing of Spiritual Terrorism/Insanity

After the publication of *Spiritual Terrorism*, Jay, from Australia, contacted me to say that he desperately needed help. He explained that he had been the caregiver for his father who was a hospice patient. His father, who was a good man but not a Christian, had died. Jay, growing up in a Christian Church, had been taught that all people who do not personally accept Christ before they die will be tormented in hell fire forever—no exceptions and no second chances. Jay further shared with me that after his beloved father had died, he became so depressed, thinking and worrying about his father being tormented in hell eternally, that he became physically dysfunctional and had to be admitted to a psychiatric hospital.

In the hospital, Jay told the doctors the cause of his depression and dysfunctionality. They medicated him, gave him some talk therapy, and discharged him with the instructions to do deep-breathing exercises and meditate. How could he have meditated while being tormented with thoughts and visual imagery of his beloved father being tortured in hell fire forever? Thus, Jay was still very depressed and again becoming physically dysfunctional!

I asked Jay how he had gotten my name and contact information from way "down under" in Australia. He explained that he, while worrying about needing to be re-hospitalized for psychiatric treatment, was trying to think of words which would describe what he had been so painfully experiencing, and two words came to mind—"spiritual terrorism!" He Googled those two words and my website: HealingSpiritualTerrorism.com (which has contact information) was displayed on his computer screen. He got my book and read it finding peace with God, tranquility of mind, healing for damaged emotions, and joy of living. He was healed of spiritual insanity which caused the terrorism. And he did not have to be re-hospitalized for psychiatric care.

Severe Depression from Reading Book on Hell

A woman, Alice, from the country of South Africa, contacted me for spiritual and psychological help due to suffering from a severe depressive state. She was a good candidate for treatment in a psychiatric hospital. Alice poured out her heart that she had been continually spiritually abused in Christian Churches from the time she was a child. She, in fact, had been so traumatized by fear of eternal torture in hell fire that she had made the decision, as a young woman, never to have children in order to not risk putting children in danger of eternal damnation.

At the time she contacted me, Alice was in her mid-40s and will die childless due to having steadfastly stuck with her decision to never bring children into this world who would have any possibility of being tortured in hell fire eternally. She was existing in an emotional hell on a daily basis and was thus in an emotionally unstable condition. In this miserable condition, she read a book titled, *23 Minutes in Hell* authored by Bill Wiese.[1] Alice was so terrified by the contents of this book that she was driven into a severe state of depression for two years! To understand how this happened, one needs to understand what Wiese penned in this book about literal [or worse] hell fire. I wrote a review of this book and posted it on Amazon.com, November 17, 2010, giving it one star of a possible five-star rating.

Being in Literal Hell Fire?

In 2006 Bill Wiese wrote the extremely popular book, *23 Minutes in Hell*, which became a New York Times best seller. This book is Wiese's reported experience of God having given him a "show and tell"—actually being in hell for 23 minutes— to let him know firsthand how horrible hell really is so he could go back and spread the word in order to save as many people as possible from eternal damnation in hell fire. Wiese, in 2008 wrote his sequel, *Hell*, which is a proof-text study of *the Bible* to find verses to substantiate his perceived experience of hell. Based on his literal interpretation of *the Bible*, he, of course, found such verses.

Wiese stated that just as the physical descriptions of heaven, such as the pearly gates and streets of gold, are literal so, likewise, the physical descriptions of the fire of hell must also be literal. The truth is that neither the physical descriptions of heaven nor hell are literal. It is all symbolic language to describe realities in the spiritual world of which words are inadequate to express.

Jesus' symbolic words, "salted with fire" (Mk. 9:49), are IMPOSSIBLE to be literal. Someone or something can be salted with salt or burned with fire, but no one or anything can be salted with fire. This is a mixed metaphor which, beyond any doubt whatsoever based on the Biblical use of salt and fire, symbolizes purification. Jesus, beyond any doubt, deliberately mixed these two Biblical symbols for purification in order to prevent literalists from logically interpreting this beautiful, timeless, cross-cultural symbolism for purification literally.

Incurable Literalists: Worse than Literal Fire!

But literalists, being who literalists are and doing what literalists do, interpret [if they have even heard of it which few have] "salted with fire" literally anyway. When curable literalists learn of being "salted with fire" they logically conclude that hell is for the purpose of purification. Wiese proved himself to be an incurable literalist when he said that the fire of hell, if not literal symbolizes something worse than literal fire. This contention is absolute nonsense! If "worse than literal fire" is to the human spirit what literal fire is to the human body, it cannot be worse! No, it symbolizes something infinitely better—purification!

Ironically, in a perverse way, Wiese argues for metaphorical fire in that he contends that hell is deep in the earth (core 12,000 degrees), and God will intensify this heat of literal fire in order to make hell even more torturous for the vast majority of the world who will be condemned to the eternal fire. This even includes the billions of people (including infants, all of whom are guilty of original sin, per the late John Gerstner whose theology Wiese referenced) who died without ever having heard about salvation in Christ who is the only way to heaven.

But, according to Wiese, God is very saddened by having to condemn so many people to eternal damnation EVEN THOUGH HE LOVES THEM! If God tortures people forever in hell fire, what difference does it make if He loves them? God might as well hate them; the result would be no different!

Spiritual Schizophrenia

Wiese's "reasoning" that sinners cause God to punish them in hell fire forever is a good example of spiritual schizophrenia. Dr. Kirby Godsey, a former Southern Baptist college president, wrote an excellent book in favor of Christian Universalism, *When We Talk About God...Let's Be Honest.*[2] So let's be honest in talking about God. To say that sinners force God to torture them forever in fire which is even hotter than literal fire, is a pathetic excuse for God doing something unbelievably sadistic! Wiese clearly believes in a god who is a spiritual schizophrenic. That is, God desires all people to be saved, but, even though God is omniscient, He is not smart enough to figure out a way to bring all sinners around to doing His will without violating their free will.

Inescapable Love/Irresistible Grace

The solution to that theological problem, of God's sovereignty vs. human free will, is called, the "Inescapable love of God" [see chapter 10] or "irresistible grace," which means although God's saving grace can be resisted indefinitely, it will not be resisted forever. Since God is also omnipotent, He has the power as well as unconditional love to out love and out last sinners until the last prodigal son or daughter comes home to heaven where there will be great rejoicing. Jesus said, in the Parable of the Good Shepherd, there will be more rejoicing over one sinner who repents than over 99 persons who did not need to repent (Luke 15:7)!

Jesus declared that He came to save the lost. He stated that the good shepherd searched for his one lost sheep *until he found it*. This is the same parable He told in Luke 15:3-7 with the added information of Him coming to save the lost and it not being the Father's will for even one little one to perish (Mt. 18:11-14). Robert Rutherford, who believes in Christian Universalism, wrote this poem, posted on Facebook [used with his permission].

The Missing Part

If a deck of cards has only 51 cards,
you cannot play the game.
If a girl has all her teeth except one missing
in the front, she doesn't look the same.
If your kids come home for Christmas and
only one stays away, your thoughts will be
for that missing one most all the day.
It's the missing part that will grab your heart
a card, a tooth, a son...that's why he left the
Ninety nine and went and found the one.

As long as even one sinner is estranged from God, that one is a missing part of the family of God. Therefore, God will be grieved, since He cannot be all in all (KJV)—everything to every one (I Cor. 15:28 RSV) until He finds the one! God, is omnipresent and a "consuming fire" (Ps. 139:7, 8; Deut. 4:24; Heb. 12:29), who will find and purify all sinners. He will not torture sinners at all, much less forever! This reveals Christian Universalism to be the Biblical truth and exposes the doctrine of eternal torture for the big lie, "from the pit of hell" [as literalists say], it is!

Criminal as well as Spiritual Insanity

It was via the writings of the Christian writer George MacDonald (1824-1905), who believed in CU, that atheist C.S. Lewis (1898-1963) came to believe in Christ. On the cover of the book, *George MacDonald*, is a quote of C.S. Lewis. "I have never concealed the fact that I regarded him as my master."[3] Lewis also said he knew of no writer, "...so continuously close to the Spirit of Christ."[4] MacDonald said that if people of the world believed in eternal torment in hell fire, half of the world would be insane while the other half would be atheists! Of literalists belief in eternal/literal hell fire, it can be said with certainty that their version of Christianity is spiritual insanity, and their god is criminally insane!

Those who believe it are at risk of mental as well as spiritual insanity. It is child abuse and is often the basis of (no divorce at all or only for adultery) spousal abuse. Such terroristic theology, which frightens people into accepting Christ as their Savior, also locks them into a state of perpetual spiritual infancy and causes spiritual insanity.

Fearing: Reverence/Sense of Awe

Yes, *the Bible* says in Proverbs that fear of the Lord is the beginning of wisdom. But note that such fear is only the "beginning." *The Bible* says in *the New Testament* that the one who fears is not perfected in love because fear is torment; perfect love casts out fear. Biblical fear means a reverence for or a sense of awe about God, not morbid fear. The Apostle Peter admonished new believers to grow in the grace and knowledge of our Lord and Savior Jesus Christ (II Peter 3:18).

But believers can never grow spiritually in an atmosphere of fear. In order for Christians to grow spiritually, if they have been scared into accepting Christ, that initial fear must be transformed into a love relationship which will happen only when they have come to understand God's unconditional and everlasting love, amazing grace, infinite mercy and patience, and perfect justice.

Christianity Without Insanity

For Christianity without insanity, read good books that expose the false doctrine of eternal punishment as spiritual insanity and Christian Universalism as the glorious truth which it certainly is! This totally positive conception of God elicits love of God, enhances worship of God, and promotes altruistic service for God in addition to optimizing emotional, mental, spiritual, and even physical health!

Ex-Christian to Christian Universalist

Alice, the lady from South Africa, purchased my book, read it, and found the peace which surpasses human understanding! She did not need to be hospitalized for psychiatric treatment. Alice was so blessed by my book she wrote a five-star review of *Spiritual Terrorism* and posted it on Amazon.com [can read whole review]. Here are excerpts from her ["a Woman on a Mission"] review:

> It was by sheer chance that I came across this book as I was actually looking for something else, at the time I was trying to break free of Christianity altogether, but could not become convinced that there wasn't a God. Fortunately Dr. Purcell says belief in the doctrine of eternal torment is not the litmus test to determine whether one is a Christian... some even making the outrageous claim that it [eternal torture] glorifies God; how and why I could never know, how such an unspeakable nightmare could even begin to be good news is unfathomable.
>
> Why this book was so important to me personally, is that Dr. Purcell has hands on experience in dealing with people who have been spiritually terrorized as he worked as a hospice chaplain for many years....He shows universalism in Christianity....and also shows universalism in [all major] religions. The remedial and metaphorical view of hell (which is temporary) makes perfect sense....I intend to read it again. I can't thank the author enough for what he has written; I think this book is worth every penny and more!!!!

The "something else" Alice was looking for was the website: "**exchristian.net**." If doubting the need for my book, Google this website. She had "deconverted" from Christianity and joined this online group of very angry former Christians who have been terrorized due to spiritual insanity. After reading my book, Alice left that group and is now calling herself a "Christian Universalist!"

Who is the Insane One?

In their excellent book, *Good Goats: Healing Our Image of God,* Catholic authors, Dennis, Matthew, and Sheila Linn, addressed the tragic case of a man who had been admitted to a psychiatric ward due to having attempted to gouge out his eyes based on a literal understanding of Jesus saying it would be better to cut off one's hand or foot or gouge out one's eyes than to go into hell (Mark 9:43-49). They insightfully asked, is the crazy one the person who believes in eternal torment but isn't willing to mutilate one's body in order to avoid going there or the one who takes eternal torture so seriously as to actually cut off one's hands or feet or gouge out one's eyes to stay out of eternal hell fire at all cost?[5]

Hell Fire Literal but not Bodily Mutilation?

Readers, what about you? Are you a "Bible-believing" Christian? If so, do you believe *the Bible* must be interpreted literally and that, as some "Bible-believing" Christians claim, every word in *the Bible* is literally true? Why do almost all Biblical literalists take the fire of hell literally but not the bodily mutilation literally? This kind of spiritual insanity is an infrequent but unnecessary tragic happening. Various Internet news sites posted this horrific story which happened on Sunday, October 2, 2011, in Viareggio, Italy. Aldo Bianchini, a 46-year-old man, blinded himself and traumatized worshipers attending mass at Saint Andrea Catholic Church when he suddenly stood up, tore out his eyes from their sockets with his bare hands, then collapsed in a pool of blood. He was rushed to the hospital, but the doctors were not able to save his sight.

SPIRITUAL ADHD

Some children have a learning disorder called ADHD which is Attention Deficit Hyperactivity Disorder. This condition is far worse than children just being normal and active. ADHD can cause serious learning problems. Although some children may be misdiagnosed and over medicated, many children do well if they are properly medicated by a physician and have family therapy.

But there is another serious condition affecting adults which almost always goes undiagnosed and untreated and potentially causes debilitating mental, emotional, and physical problems. This is not to be found in the therapist's "bible," *The Diagnostic and Statistical Manual of Mental Disorder—IV*. I have termed this condition, "Spiritual ADHD" which is, "Afraid of Death Health-Destroying Disorder," especially due to "The One Great Phobia."

The One Great Phobia

Phobia is from the Greek word "phobos," which means fear. Humans have at least one phobia. Many have more than one, and some people have multiple phobias. Some of the more common phobias are: acrophobia (fear of heights), agoraphobia (fear of public places), algophobia (fear of pain), claustrophobia (fear of closed spaces), hemophobia (fear of blood), mysophobia (fear of dirt/germs), pathophobia (fear of disease), and xenophobia (fear of strangers). Panophobia, not common, is fear of everything. Some clinicians have theorized that all phobias are just different manifestations of one primary phobia—the mother of all phobias.

Irvin D. Yalom, M.D., Professor of Psychiatry Emeritus, at Stanford University, in 2008, after *Spiritual Terrorism* was published, wrote a fascinating book, *Staring at the Sun: Overcoming the Terror of Death.*[6] Yalom's thesis is that just as a person cannot stare at the sun without being physically blinded, so one cannot stare at death without being emotionally blinded. Based on his lifetime work of studying fear of death and helping people deal with their phobias, there is One Great Phobia—**fear of death!**

Yalom being an atheist does not invalidate his medical research and expertise. Atheism may be an intellectual issue, but it is often a reaction to and a defense against the god of fear-based religion. Yalom said, "Death anxiety is the mother of all religions...."[7] Such religion causes agnosticism, atheism, cynicism, and skepticism.

According to Yalom, **"Death anxiety is omnipresent in the unconscious as an intrinsic component of the human condition; the absence of evident death anxiety at a conscious level does not mean that the individual is without death anxiety; death anxiety is easily aroused."** He explained that for some people, death anxiety is in the background—corralled in the unconscious mind. "But for other people, the anxiety is louder, unruly, **tending to erupt at three in the morning,** leaving them gasping at the specter of death. They are besieged by the thought that they, too, will soon be dead—as will everyone around them...Thoughts of death may seep into and permeate your dreams no matter how hidden from your conscious mind. **Every nightmare is a dream in which death anxiety has escaped its corral and menaces the dreamer"[8]** (bold mine). Yalom also said, "Anxiety about nothing [in particular as in General Anxiety D/O] is anxiety about death."[9]

In other research, the presence of death anxiety in the unconscious mind was demonstrated in a scientific study of two groups of people using the Galvanic Skin Response Test (GSR). One group of non-religious persons reported having no fear of death and never even thought about death while the other group of religious persons reported having fear of death. GSR electrodes were attached to each person to measure vital responses. A list of words normally associated with death were read to each person. The result of this study: the group denying having any fear of death and never thought about death had a significantly higher level of death anxiety than the group admitting such anxiety![10]

Of utmost interest, Yalom stated that death anxiety tends to erupt at three o'clock in the morning.[11] It may be far more than coincidence that Bill Wiese, who, in 2006, wrote the New York Times best-seller book, *23 Minutes in Hell*, reported that his experience of being in hell occurred from 3:00-3:23 a.m. If not a hoax to sell a lot of books, the most logical explanation of Wiese's perceived time in hell is that his death anxiety "escaped its corral" and, combined with his visual images of literal hell fire, menaced him with a very real-hellish nightmare.

Omnipresent-death anxiety is immeasurably worsened by morbid fear of God and eternal damnation in literal hell fire. The One Great Phobia can be very effectively treated by a totally loving conception of God and a sane, sensible explanation of hell in *the Holy Bible* and other holy books. Since the publication of *Spiritual Terrorism*, I have been receiving emails from across the country and from around the world from victims of spiritual insanity reporting that they have been healed of this mental, emotional, and physical-health menace. I hope many people will find *Christianity Without Insanity* to be life transforming in that it will heal rather than worsen the fear of The One Great Phobia!

An excellent book on CU is *Hope Beyond Hell* by Gerry Beauchemin.[12] This book is so good it has my endorsement on the back of it. This author wisely addressed the stated purpose of Christ, God in human form, coming to earth. It was to free people from fear of death so that they would not live all their lives in bondage to fear of death (Heb. 2:15). Due to lack of understanding or misunderstanding of what Jesus taught about death, heaven, and hell multitudes of Christians live in fear of death and eternal hell for oneself and/or loved ones.

Unmitigated Grief over the Death of a Child

There is probably only one thing worse than the horrific fate of parents having to deal with the death of a child; that is existing— experiencing a living death—daily, almost paralyzed with fear that one's beloved child is being tortured in literal hell fire forever! One such grieving parent was a woman whom I met while giving blood [which I have done for about 50 years] at the Red Cross Donation Center about a year after *Spiritual Terrorism* was published.

At that particular time, this woman asked me what was my occupation, and I told her that I was a hospice chaplain and that I had recently had a book published. She told me that she was a Baptist and then started telling me that she had a son who had died more than 20 years ago. As she shared more of her story, tears began to roll down her cheeks. Through tears, she related that he had died suddenly in a car wreck when he was only 16 years of age. What was heart wrenching, she lamented, was that she did not know whether her son was "saved." She sobbed that she blamed herself for not having made it her business to know of his spiritual condition, and now it was too late. She daily lived in fear that her beloved son may be in hell being tormented day and night forever!

I shared with this terrified mother that hell is not literal fire. I explained that fire in *the Bible,* in regard to judgment, symbolizes purification, so hell is not forever. When I assured her that her son is in heaven waiting for her, she was overjoyed! She stated that she had attended a Baptist Church since she was a child and had never heard this Good News. She said that she was eager to get my book and read it in order to learn more about this all-loving view of God.

Anxiety Disorders

There are various anxiety disorders. *The Diagnostic and Statistical Manual of Mental Disorders—IV*[13] has devoted over 50 pages to these mental/emotional afflictions. Two of the most common and troublesome are Obsessive-Compulsive Disorder (OCD) and Panic Disorder. There are various manifestations of these disorders, but all are anxiety driven caused by stress.

Common manifestations of OCD, repetitive behaviors, are: habitual hand washing, counting, checking, praying, clicking, avoiding, repeating actions/words, etc. The classic avoidance example is not stepping on a crack per the old saying, "If you step on a crack, you break your mother's back." These behaviors are to prevent or reduce distress from some dreaded event, may be only imagined. A great film on OCD is "As Good as it Gets," starring Jack Nicholson and Helen Hunt. On TV, "Monk" is a classic case.

One of the clients in my private counseling practice was Marge, a very intelligent, well-educated woman who was a health-care professional. In doing her mental-health history, Marge shared that she had suffered from OCD since she was a child. Her OCD manifested as fear of crossing bridges. That was not so bad when, as a child, she could close her eyes as her parent was driving over a bridge. But when she started to drive, it became problematic and greatly restricted her driving. This would not have been so bad if Marge lived in an area with few bridges, but she lived in a river valley, at the confluence of two rivers, so there was a bridge almost any place she wanted to go outside her neighborhood.

Marge finally made up her mind to get professional help. As we explored her background, she shared that she had grown up in an Evangelical Church in which the pastor preached a strong dose of eternal hell fire for all who have not accepted Christ as their Lord and Savior before death. Marge remembered that she always felt terrible about all the people in the whole world who would be tormented in hell fire forever. She stated that she was never able to sleep on Sunday nights thinking about this spiritual holocaust! She was a very loving, caring, and compassionate person who said that she still worried much about the eternal damnation of the masses of people who are not Christians. When I shared with her the truth of Christian Universalism, she did not think that it is too good to be true, as some say. She thought that it was incredibly Good News!

A Terrible Truth or God's Unconditional Love?

At that time, I had written an unpublished paper on CU, "Salted with Fire: A Terrible Truth or the Extent of God's Unconditional Love in Action?" She read it, looked up verses in *the Bible*, and seriously studied this subject to determine its validity for herself. Within a few months, she came to the joyous conclusion that the Bible actually does teach universal salvation. As Marge read and studied, her OCD lessened and then disappeared, so she was able to drive whenever and wherever she wanted to go. Just as Jesus said, she came to know the truth of God's love for all people, and the truth set her free of the anxiety, from fear, causing her OCD.

Panic Disorder is a huge problem in the USA. In *Spiritual Terrorism*, I devoted a whole chapter, "The Ultimate Dilemma," to this mental-health menace.[14] I described the ultimate dilemma as at first being afraid you are going to die but being in such mental/emotional pain you are afraid you won't die! Millions of people suffer from this problem, but most people who have Panic Disorder are not aware that they have it. The reason that we have such a widespread problem of alcohol, illegal drugs, and the abuse of prescription medications is most likely due to the unfortunate people, who have this anxiety affliction, trying to self-medicate.

I have worked at a substance-abuse rehabilitation inpatient and outpatient center. The literature on substance abuse estimates that as many as 75-80 percent of substance abusers suffer from Panic Disorder! This is why "Just say, 'No,'" substance-abuse programs do not work. People know that drugs are not good for them, but they also know that panic symptoms are worse for them. They drink and/or use drugs to try to keep anxiety under control and feel normal. Those who want more information may want to read *Spiritual Terrorism* in which I listed all 13 systems of Panic Disorder in *the DSM—IV*. The most frightening symptoms are pounding heart, smothering sensations, shaking, choking, fear of losing control, fear of going crazy, and fear of dying.

I have found that anxiety caused by fear of death and eternal torture in literal hell fire is frequently the driving force behind panic symptoms. When victims of spiritual insanity learn that they are unconditionally loved by God, that hell is for purification, and all people will eventually be purified, reconciled, and restored to God, their panic symptoms have diminished and then disappeared [including addictive behaviors]. Psalm 23 is a wonderful expression of peace with the Lord being our shepherd. It is the opposite of what people experience who have Panic Disorder. I have rewritten Psalm 23 from the perspective of one who suffers from "The Ultimate Dilemma." It is to help them get from where they are to where they want and need to be with God.

"Panic Disorder is my shepherd; I shall want but have no hope. Thou maketh me to fall down in pastures of nervous exhaustion. Thou leadeth me beside the troubled waters of addiction and misery. Thou destroyeth my soul with panic attacks through feeling trapped. Thou leadeth me in the paths of helplessness and hopelessness for no purpose's sake. Yea, I walk through the valley of the shadow of death, fearing all evil: For thou art with me; thy rod of racing heart and staff of smothering sensations discomfort me. Thou preparest a trap for me in the presence of my emotional enemies—feelings of choking, chills, shaking, sweating, faintness, numbness, nausea, detachment from my body, and a sense of unreality. Thou anointest my head with despair; my cup of anxiety runneth over. Surely fear of going crazy and dying shall stalk me all days of my life; And I will dwell in the house of the damned forever."

My paraphrase of the 23rd Psalm may seem extreme to those who have never experienced the terror of Panic Disorder. But victims of panic attacks have expressed their opinion that it is very descriptive of their ordeal, since panic is an extreme nervous reaction. Jane, from the state of Alabama, sent me several emails expressing her thanks for the insight she gained about the cause of her panic attacks from reading *Spiritual Terrorism*. She sent the email below and then wrote and posted a five-star review of my book on Amazon.com. Sadly, her husband not only refused to read my book, apparently, he later coerced her into deleting her review. He needs to be aware that his controlling behavior may well put her back into panic attacks.

Spiritual Healing

Your book has been such a blessing to me. Two years ago I had a breakdown, started having panic attacks and thought I was losing my mind. This all started after I attended a bible study at church about heaven, but of course, you can't have a study about heaven without talking about hell. The things I read and the things that were being said seemed absurd to me, and I started to question the eternal punishment doctrine. To make a long story short, I was on antidepressants and sleeping pills for about a year, and even then had difficulty functioning. I am finally free, now that I know Jesus really is the savior of the world! Your book hit the nail on the head! I have been a believer in Universal Salvation for the past two years, but after reading your book, I have a much better understanding of what caused the panic attacks and the extreme anxiety I was experiencing. I knew before that it was spiritual, but thought I was at fault for "questioning the word of God," even though I had prayed in earnest for answers to my very valid questions. When God led me to the answers, it really upset my apple cart! Please pray for me, my husband's eyes have not yet been opened. We are still attending the same church, where he is an officer and bible study teacher. I do not want to embarrass him, but I feel like a phony for not speaking up about what I believe. I want him to read your book, but he is resistant to do so. Thank you again....I finally feel like I have been set free.

Health Benefit of Positive Spirituality

As shown in this book, fearful images of God and fear of eternal damnation in hell fire can have profoundly negative consequences on people's health. On the positive side, what does *the Bible* say about the positive benefits of a loving, caring conception of God? Actually, there is quite a bit. Consider what strong positive emotions would be generated by belief in God as portrayed by these Biblical images of God. It has been said that it is easy for people to believe in God [as almost all people do], but it is hard to trust God. These words of wisdom from Hebrew and Christian sacred writings, spoken by the holy prophets and apostles, instill trust in God, not just belief in God. Such wonderful truth inspires trust, faith, hope, and love that optimizes spiritual/mental/emotional/physical health!

The Old Testament

From *the Old Testament*, we have these comforting Scriptures for the people of Israel and, by extension since God is impartial, all

39

people of the world (Rom. 2:11). Isaiah says, "The Lord will keep one in perfect peace whose mind is stayed on Him, due to trusting in Him. Trust in the Lord forever, for in the Lord God is everlasting strength" (26:3, 4). Jeremiah stated, "The steadfast love of the Lord never ceases, God's mercies never come to an end; they are new every morning; great is His faithfulness" (Lam. 3:22, 23). Proverbs wisely counsels: "Trust in the Lord with all your heart and lean not unto your own understanding; in all yours ways acknowledge Him, and He shall direct your paths (3:5, 6). When people's ways please the Lord, He will even make their enemies to be at peace with them (Prov. 16:7). As people think in their heart [symbolic seat of emotions], so they are" [as whole or fractured persons due to mind/body connection] (Prov. 23:7).

The Psalmist uttered two rhetorical questions of profoundly comforting truth: "The Lord is my light and my salvation; whom [or what] shall I fear? The Lord is the strength of my life; of whom [or what] shall I be afraid?...I had fainted, unless I had believed to see the goodness of the Lord in the land of the living. Wait on the Lord: be of good courage, and he shall strengthen your heart: wait, I say, on the Lord." (27:1, 13, 14). This priestly blessing has been comforting to Jews throughout the centuries and as a benediction for Christians for over 2,000 years and still is in many churches today. "The Lord bless you and keep you, the Lord make His face to shine upon you, and be gracious unto you. The Lord lift up His countenance upon you, and give you peace" (Num. 6:24-26).

The Teachings of Jesus

In regard to all the problems of life, Jesus consistently admonished His followers not to worry. His wise words were to live in the present, not to worry about what might or might not happen the next day, "Do not worry about tomorrow for today has enough worries of its own." In regard to worrying about the necessities of life, Jesus counseled, "Since God clothes the lilies of the field and feeds the birds of the air, how much more will He cloth and feed you. You cannot add an inch to your height nor a day to your life by worrying, so do not worry" (Mt. 6:25-34).

When His disciples were fearful, he exhorted them not to fear (Mt. 8:26). He instilled peace in His disciples: "Peace I leave with you, my peace I give unto you: not as the world gives, but as I give unto you. Let not your heart be troubled, neither let it be afraid" (John 14:27). Jesus' parting words of comfort were: "I will be with you always, even to the end of the world" [KJV] (Mt. 28:20).

The Apostle Paul

The Apostle Paul instilled peace of mind in Christians at Rome. "Therefore, being justified by faith, we have peace with God through our Lord Jesus Christ" (5:1). "Do not be conformed to this world, but be transformed by the renewing of your mind, that you may prove what is that good, and acceptable, and perfect will of God" (Rom. 12:2). Paul discipled the Christians at Galatia to be filled with the Holy Spirit in order to manifest the fruit of the Holy Spirit: "The fruit of the Spirit is love, joy, peace, patience, gentleness, goodness, faith, meekness, and self control" (5:22, 23). To the church at Philippi, Paul calmed their fears: "Do not be anxious about anything, but in everything by prayer and petition with thanksgiving let your requests be made known unto God. And the peace of God, which exceeds all understanding, shall keep your hearts and minds through Christ Jesus" (4:6, 7).

"Finally, brethren, whatsoever things are true, honest, just, pure, lovely, of good report, if there is any virtue and praise, think on these things...and the God of peace shall be with you" (Phil. 4:8, 9). To Timothy, Paul wrote: "For God has not given us the spirit of fear, but of power, and of love, and of a sound mind" (II Tim. 1:7). To the believers at Colossae Paul admonished: "Above all, put on love, which is the bond of perfection, and let the peace of God rule in your hearts..." (3:14, 15).

The Apostles Peter and John and Writer of Hebrews

The Apostle Peter penned these comforting words: "Cast all your cares on Him, for He cares for you" (I Peter 5:7). And "Grace and peace be multiplied unto you through the knowledge of God, and of Jesus our Lord" (II Peter 1:2). After giving one of the four Biblical definitions of God—"God is love" (I John 4:8)—the Apostle John went on to declare: "The one who fears is not perfected in love; because fear is torment. Perfect love casts out fear" (4:18). God's love—"agape" (I Cor. 13)—is perfect love. The writer of Hebrews explained the implications of the Lord being our helper: "He [Jesus] has said, 'I will never leave you, nor forsake you.' So we may boldly say, the Lord is my helper, and I will not fear what people shall do unto me" (13:5, 6). Thus, God helps, not harms us!

The Apostle John captured the essence of the dynamics of psychopathology in these comforting, encouraging, and inspiring words: "Beloved, I wish above all things that you may prosper and be in health, even as your soul prospers" (III John 2). The truth is no person's soul can prosper, and, therefore, no one can be in optimal mental/emotional/physical health if living in fear of eternal torture in hell for oneself and/or loved ones.

Neurophysiology and Neurotheology

A very exciting area of scientific research is the field of Neurophysiology which deals with research, diagnosis, and treatment of anxiety disorders. It addresses the comprehensive effects of stress from various sources including spiritual, caused by anxiety, and its impact on the brain, immune system, and body as a whole.

A relatively new area of scientific research is Neurotheology which uses the methods of neuroscience to study the impact praying, meditating, and doing positive thinking have on specific areas of the brain and how they impact the whole person. Neurotheology also includes the reaction of the brain and its impact on one's body to negative emotions elicited by fear-based religion, such as: anger, resentment, bitterness, hatred and fear of living, dying, judgment, hell, etc. Much more information is online.

Discussion Questions

1. What is the basic premise of psychopathology?

2. Does it make sense to use a "/" between the words: spiritual/mental/emotional/physical health. Why? If not, why not?

3. How does this holistic approach to health optimize people's well being?

4. What did Jesus mean by saying that as a person thinks in one's heart so he or she is?

5. What do you understand about the fact that a person's nervous system is unable to distinguish the difference between something actually happening and something vividly imagined?

6. The Apostle Paul wrote, "Be not conformed to this world, but be transformed by the renewing of your mind..." (Rom. 12:2). How does Jay illustrate this truth?

7. Paul also stated, "Think on the things which are right, good, and are of a good report, and the God of peace will be with you." How does Alice's situation show the opposite— morbid thinking and no peace?

8. If the doctrine of eternal torture in hell is true, would amputating one's extremities and blinding oneself be worth it, and even a relatively small price to pay, to not be condemned to hell for eternity? What is wrong with this picture? What does common sense dictate?

9. What do you understand about Neurophysiology and Neurotheology and implications for health?

Chapter 3
Religions of the World

The "R" in the acrostic "CHRISTIANITY" represents "World Religions," major and minor ones, teaching ultimate oneness with the One Supreme Being. Religion has been one of the most divisive and destructive forces in the history of the world. But, as the world increasingly becomes a global village, religion needs to become a great unifying force for good. When religious people universally understand that all major religions and most, if not all, minor ones teach universal salvation, religion will become the greatest unifying force for good the world has ever seen. Religion will thus, eventually, have a greater impact on the world than the discovery of fire, since this will be spiritual fire!

Yes, there are significant differences between world religions, but there are many similarities. The focus of this chapter is on the similarities, not the differences. This chapter explores the commonalities of symbolic-religious language in *The Holy Bible* as well as the sacred writings in other religions, except for the use of the word "fire." Fire is a very significant religious symbol. Interpreted literally, fire has thus caused untold pain and suffering. I have, therefore, devoted chapter five, "Symbolism of Fire," to it.

Ultimate Victory of Good over Evil

The ultimate victory of good over evil is the yearning of every one of good will. Eventually, there will be no people of bad will when all have willingly submitted to God's unconditional love and are harmoniously living with God and in peace with every other created being in the whole universe. It is presently the blessed hope; some splendid day it will be a glorious reality!

In theological terms, Webster defines "universalism" as the doctrine that all people will eventually be saved. The dictionary definition, however, does not specify how that is going to happen.

Major religions express it differently, but all of them, in their essence, teach universal salvation. The doctrine of divine punishment, in general and eternal punishment in particular, has been used to control people in various religious faiths. At best, this is spiritual abuse; at worst, it is spiritual terrorism. Some have asked if it is spiritual abuse if it is unintentional. It is spiritually abusive either way, but intentional abuse makes the responsibility and culpability of the religious abuser far worse. It is hurtful and abusive whether it is called spiritual terrorism or spiritual insanity.

God is Love

All religions describe God as a God of love. In Christianity, one of the four Biblical definitions of God is "God is Love" (I John 4:8). I agree with Gerald May, M.D., a psychiatrist who wrote an excellent book, *Addiction and Grace*. He explained addiction based on the models of medical, physiological, psychological, and spiritual perspectives. May said that grace is the most powerful force in the universe, because it is divine love in action![1]

God's love is all inclusive, since it includes all and excludes none. Thus, because God's love is unconditional, there are absolutely no conditions for it! Since it is everlasting, God will never stop loving anyone—even those while still in hell.

God Hating and Christians Hating Others?

Even though religions as a whole characterize God as being love, there are problematic passages in sacred writings which superficially appear to contradict this truth. In holy books, some things may, on the surface, appear to be contradictions. For example, God said to the people of Israel, through Jeremiah the prophet, that He loved them with everlasting love. He, therefore, had drawn them with lovingkindness (31:3). Thus, God's love would appear to be unconditional and everlasting. Yet *the Torah* records that God also said that He had loved Jacob but hated Esau (Mal. 1:1-3). This was in regard to Esau bartering his birthright to Jacob for a bowl of soup. Granted, this was a thoughtless act, but

45

did it warrant God's love turning to hate? Love never fails (I Cor. 13:8). *It is, therefore, impossible for God's love to fail. It is also impossible to hate one's family as well as oneself, in order to be Jesus' disciple (Luke 14:26), and then love others as oneself (Mt. 22:34-40). Biblical commands to hate are not to be taken literally.*

Dr. Rocco Errico, who has devoted his life to studying the Aramaic Language which Jesus spoke, ordained by the Unity Church, has written several books. Two of Errico's books are: *And There Was Light* and *Let There Be Light,* both of which are excellent. In *Let There Be Light*[2] he explained that in Aramaic the word "hate" has multiple meanings. Depending on the context, it can mean a strong dislike or to "put to one side." The latter appears to be the meaning in regard to God "hating" Esau. After selling his birthright to his brother Jacob, God put him aside [due to Esau putting himself aside], out of the messianic lineage, and Jacob became the line through whom the Messiah would come. I stated in *Spiritual Terrorism* that God did not treat Esau badly. In fact, as Esau testified years later at his homecoming with Jacob, God had blessed him in having an abundance of material things (Gen. 33:9).

In *the Holy Koran* there are two verses which appear to be problematic in relation to God's love. "Say: "If ye do love Allah, follow me; Allah will love you and forgive you your sins: for Allah is Oft-Forgiving, Most Merciful" (3:31). But the next verse declares, "Say: "Obey Allah and His Messenger: but if they turn back, Allah loveth not those who reject Faith" (3:32).

In *the Holy Bible* we have the same problem of understanding God's love. Even the definition "God is love" appears to be contradicted by the multiple reasons for which people will be cast into hell fire *if the doctrine of eternal punishment is true*: "He who overcomes will inherit all this, and I will be his God and he will be my son. But the cowardly, the unbelieving, the vile, the murderers, the sexually immoral, those who practice magic arts, the idolaters and all liars—their place will be in the fiery lake of burning sulfur" (Rev. 21:7, 8 NIV). God's unconditional love and everlasting love vs. eternal torment are two of the top ten oxymorons [in chapter 1].

46

Calvinism

The term "Calvinism" refers to the theology of the Protestant reformer, John Calvin (1509-1564). Dr. Bill Evans is the author of an Adult Sunday School Quarterly which is a publication of the Associate Reformed Presbyterian Church. In the lesson for March 25, 2012, on John 3:16, Evans said the term "world" is used qualitatively rather than quantitatively to refer to all kinds of human beings as they are in rebellion against God. It does not mean "all human beings without exception." Why? Evans stated, "God sent his Son, not to condemn the world, but to save the world (here, incidentally, we see that interpreting the term 'world' as meaning all people without exception would result in a doctrine of universal salvation, something clearly contradicted in Scripture)."[3]

No, universal salvation is not clearly contradicted in the Holy Scriptures. Actually, the opposite is true! Universal salvation is clearly, unambiguously, and unequivocally taught in *the Holy Bible* from Genesis to the Revelation. So how did Dr. Evans and other Biblical commentators get it so wrong? Evans is representative of those who identify themselves as Calvinists—those who believe God only loves the "elect," Christ only died for the "elect," and only the "elect" will be saved, because only the "elect" can be saved. Thus, any time *the Bible* says God loves the world they mentally amend it to mean, "the world 'of the elect.'" Rather than Christ drawing all people to Himself (John 12:32), they amend His words to mean, "draw all 'the elect' or all 'kinds of people' [the elect] to Himself." Such revisionism goes on in the Scriptures due to belief in the false doctrine of eternal punishment.

Is God Partial or Impartial?

If Evans and other Calvinists are right, that means God is very partial. I did a study on "partiality" and here are a few verses on what *the Bible* says about God showing no favoritism. "For there is no partiality with God" (Rom. 2:11). "Peter said, 'I most certainly understand now that God is not one to show partiality....'" (Acts 10:34). "God shows no partiality" (Gal. 2:6 New American

Standard, [NAS]). "...And there is no partiality with Him" [God, our Master in heaven] (Eph. 6:9 NAS). "...address as Father the One who impartially judges." (I Peter 1:17). Since God does not play favorites, John 3:16 is quantitative and logically teaches CU. Yes, John 3:16 seems to put the condition of "believing" on God's love. **If God puts no limit on how long unbelievers have to become believers, and if they are not coerced into believing, then God's love is truly unconditional.** But if there is a limit of this life only, including people who have never even heard of Christ, they are coerced into believing, and if God does torture people in hell forever, then God's love is definitely conditional.

Arminianism

The only other currently acceptable theological school of thought is "Arminianism," named for Jacobus Arminus (1560-1609) which teaches that God does love all without exception, Christ died for all, and God would like for all to be saved, but God's will to save is thwarted by man's free will not to accept Christ as Savior. They expound this view of God's plan of salvation in spite of the fact that *the Bible* plainly says that no plan of God can be thwarted (Job 42:2 RSV & NIV). The "T" in the acrostic "INSANITY" is for "thwarting" God's plan of salvation, which is part of the insanity in fear-based, so-called Orthodox Christianity. Since God's desire and plan is to save every one, eventually every one will be saved (I Timothy 2:3-6; II Peter 3:9).

This is the view held by the vast majority of Christians, whether Anglicans, Catholics, Orthodox, or Protestants. That all may be saved sounds good, but Arminians have also been taught and believe in the false doctrine of eternal torture. They mentally amend the Holy Scriptures to say what they think they should say, rather than believing what they do say. For example, when *the Bible* says Jesus will draw all people to Himself (John 12:32), they amend it to say, "He will 'try to draw' all people to Himself," or "all die in Adam; all live in Christ" (I Cor. 15:22), they amend it to say, "all 'kinds of people' will live in Christ." Or, they say, "all, 'who live,' live in Christ," not "all live in Christ."

48

The bottom line, whether from a Calvinistic or Arminian perspective, is that very few people are going to be saved. They both justify this terrible outcome of God's plan of salvation on a misunderstanding of what Jesus taught about the straight and narrow way and few finding the way of abundant life on earth [not eternal life in heaven] (Mt. 7:13, 14). They read the word "destruction" as hell even though the world "hell" is nowhere in these verses. They persist in reading "hell" into Jesus' teachings.

How are people to know the true nature of God's love and undefeatable plan to save every one? The answer is to think, have an open mind, and come to know the heart of God. **Believe that God loves you at least as much as the person who loves you the most. Thus, hell is God's totally effective, cosmic-recycling center to purify all sinners and transform them into saints!**

Mysticism

Mysticism means to go beyond mere words of Scriptures to meditate about God, understand the heart of God, and seek to become as loving as God. There have been and are mystics in every religion. In Judaism the branch of mysticism is Kabbalah. John the Baptist, who lived in the desert, dressed in camel-hair clothes, had a humble diet of locusts and wild honey and preached the path to peace with God, would be considered a Jewish mystic (Mt. 3:1-12) He, of course, baptized Jesus (vv. 13-17).

In Islam mysticism is seen in Sufism. The Arabic word "suf," from which the words "Sufi/Sufism" come, means "wool." Islamic mystics dressed simply in coarse-woolen garments. Gandhi, in Hinduism, would be considered a mystic. A prince, Siddharta Gautama, the founder of Buddhism, forsook a life of privilege and lived a life of poverty and meditation to find the path to oneness with God. Mystics have been misunderstood, since they have often not lived, looked, dressed, thought, or acted conventionally. Mystics have been considered great men and women of God.

In early Christianity the Gnostics were mystics. Gnosticism was later condemned as a heresy, but mysticism continued. Mysticism has had a long history in Christianity in general and the Roman Catholic and Orthodox Churches in particular. Saint John of the Cross is a well-known Catholic mystic. Mystic Christians and those of other religions have often withdrawn from the world, dressed simply, meditated, and taught the path to peace with God.

Mystics have understood metaphorical language, religious symbolism, and the fact that a loving God cannot torture people at all, much less forever. They have, accordingly, had a totally loving view of God and belief in universal salvation. The noble truth that worship of God should be out of pure love and desire for oneness with God is essentially the message of the mystics of all religions throughout the ages.

The discovery of the Dead Sea Scrolls shed a "flood of light" on the brotherhood of the Essenes, a monastic brotherhood of mystics, who lived at Qumran near the shore of the Dead Sea.[4] Per church history, some Christian scholars believe that Jesus may have studied, meditated, and worshiped with the Essenes between the ages of 12-30 (the silent years) until he began his public ministry. Jesus stated that the first and foremost commandment is to love God with all your heart, soul, and mind (Mt. 22:37). No person can love God with one's mind and believe in eternal torture.

Loving with one's mind cannot happen while motivated by fear of God, because fear and love cannot co-exist! Fear is torment, but perfect love casts out fear (I John 4:8, 18). God's goal is to perfect every one in His unconditional eternal love.

A Crisis of Faith

As virtually everyone knows, Mother Teresa was a Catholic who dedicated her life to serving the poorest of the poor in India. Her life is a great example of the love of Christ in action. But, as reported in the media in the summer of 2007, Mother Teresa had a crisis of faith—even questioning the existence of God! It may have been for other reasons, but a crisis of faith would be a normal response of a Christian whose church teaches the doctrine of eternal damnation for all who do not confess faith in Christ in this life. Those who work closely with people of non-Christian faiths, and love these people as themselves, cannot conceive that God will torture these people forever.

My question of utmost significance is, "Does God love all people as He loves Himself?" If so, how can God torture anyone at all much less forever? Logic dictates that God, who is love, created all people in love and will, in love, save ALL!

Any thinking Christian, who believes in the doctrine of eternal punishment in hell fire for all people who do not accept Christ in this life, will inevitably question the love of God, the justice of God, or even the existence of God!

Perhaps the message of Christian universal salvation would have resolved Mother Teresa's doubts as it has for others. It is one thing to consign the nameless, faceless multitudes of non-Christians to eternal perdition, but it is entirely another matter to do so to the same people after having met them face-to-face and having gotten to know them by name! God does not want us to unquestioningly accept a hand-me-down religious doctrine such as eternal punishment which defies logic. Since it defies logic, this is part of the insanity in so-called Orthodox Christianity.

To illustrate the point about defying logic, an official in an Evangelical denomination, Louis King, conceded that the "truth" of the doctrine of eternal punishment cannot be arrived at either by deduction or induction—the only two ways human beings have, other than personal experience, of learning anything. King concluded that, therefore, the doctrine of eternal punishment is a revelation of God.[5] This means that, *if this doctrine is true*, God has given humans an irrational revelation. That is, without a doubt, absolute nonsense, spiritual terrorism, and spiritual insanity!

51

God is Light

"God is Light" is one of the four Biblical definitions of God (I John 1:5). Light is a common religious symbol for the Eternal One. A common theme in religious literature is the battle of the Light against the forces of spiritual darkness. Believers are called "Children of Light" and the "Light of the World."

The Eastern Religions

Light is a significant symbol of God in the Eastern as well as Western religions. God is often symbolized as Light in the form of candles, lamps, halos, auras, and flames. Light is a very appropriate symbol for conveying spiritual truths. Since light is invisible, it must be depicted in visible forms in the secular as well as the sacred realm. Consider the torch of the great lady—the Statue of Liberty. Her message is, "I lift my lamp beside the golden door." Just as she lights the way to political freedom, **the Light of God lights the way to spiritual freedom!**

In Hinduism the major holiday is called "The Festival of Lights." It is also celebrated in Sikhism and Jainism. **The Festival of Lights symbolizes the ultimate victory of good over evil.** Lamps are lit in homes, as well as public places, for five consecutive days in celebration of this great future event—the hope of all mankind! It is also a time to strengthen family and other social relationships and to renounce negative feelings such as anger, envy, hatred, bitterness, greed, jealousy, etc. People are to look for the good in others, **including their enemies.**

As more and more Hindus have immigrated to other countries, The Festival of Lights is being celebrated throughout the world. It is thus a national and an international festival. People who are not members of an Eastern religion are welcome to celebrate this joyous event. The Festival of Lights can be likened to Christmas, which is a great and joyous event for Christians. Christmas is a time of many lights celebrating the birth of the Savior who will some future day destroy evil and save the whole world.

Like Christmas, The Festival of Lights is a time of exchanging gifts. The date varies, but it is always in October or November.

The victory of good over evil is also celebrated in Buddhism. Light symbolizes the enlightenment of the Buddha. Remember, the word "Buddhism" means enlightenment. Light represents the teachings of the Buddha—the enlightened one. In Buddhism, candles, lamps, or other lights are placed before shrines or other images of the Buddha. To celebrate the victory of good over evil, there is a colorful dance with masked dancers. In Buddhist Thailand, The Festival of Lights is a major event for residents as well as visitors who want to participate. It is somewhat like the "Tournament of Roses Parade" on New Year's Day in the USA; decorated floats with giant candles are paraded through the streets.

The Festival of Lights is a joyful celebration with dancers in traditional dress and musicians expressing the good news, in music and dance, of the final victory of good over evil! That is the message of all major religions and all minor ones of which I am aware. It is also the hope of the whole human race!

Inclusive or Exclusive Salvation?

Does God shine His Light only on some to the exclusion of others? Is God's Love for only a favored few but not the whole of the human family? The mystics and other godly men and women in all religious faiths have it right. God shines His Light and sends His Love for each and every person in the whole wide world. **It is interesting that the Eastern religions are inclusive of God's Light and Love, but Christianity, whose founder is "The Savior of the world"** [*if the doctrine of eternal punishment is true*], **has a very exclusive doctrine of salvation.** God forbid! Christ is indeed the Savior of the whole world! Christian Universalism honors and exalts His Holy name!

God is Spirit

God is characterized as "Spirit" in Judeo/Christianity and Islam. The Eastern Religions, as well as other religious traditions, think of God as personal Spirit while others think in terms of an impersonal force. Hinduism is more in tune with the former concept while Buddhism is more like the latter. Some have falsely accused Buddhism of being atheistic. The beliefs of Native Americans and native peoples around the world, who worship God as The Great Spirit, have significant similarities with the Eastern religions.

Almost all, if not all, religions conceptualize God as some form of Supreme Spiritual Being. In the ancient world, belief in polytheism (many gods) was predominant. Today belief in monotheism (one God) is the overwhelmingly predominant view throughout the world even though it may appear that the Eastern religions are polytheistic. All major and most, if not all, minor religions teach that every person is an eternal spirit given by God.

Question of Utmost Importance

Will all human spirits ever return to oneness with the One Eternal Spirit? If we can get past the huge problem of literalism and major superficial religious differences, the answer is, "Yes!" The Baha'i Faith, which conceptualizes God as the Divine Spirit, expresses this truth clearly, "All men have proceeded from God and unto Him shall all return."[6] The Eastern Religions believe in eventual oneness of all with God which is the ultimate purpose of reincarnations. The founder of Islam, Mohammed, said "His is the authority and to Him shall you all return" (28:88). Jesus said that he would draw all people to Himself (John 12:32).

Language is a wonderful development which facilitates human communication. But to be able to understand each other, we must be sure to grasp the meaning of words. *The Bible* says that death and life are in the power of the tongue (Proverbs 18:21).

HEALING OR DESTRUCTIVE POWER OF WORDS
"WORDS"

With words I wield destructive force
With words I can tear lives apart
With words I change history's course
With words I reveal my inner heart
Words can heal, words can destroy
Words can make us calm
Words can comfort, words can annoy
Words can be a healing balm
Miracle and curse
Praise and perverse
Words are the window of the soul....

Bobby A. Miller, II, M.D., Author of
A Christian Psychiatrist's Prayer
Emotional Healing Through Poetry[7]

In the meaning of the word "Buddhism"—God enlightenment—every one in the whole world will become Buddhist!

In the meaning of the word "Christian" like the Christ— the incarnation of God—every one in the whole world will become Christian!

In the meaning of the word "Islam"—submission to God— Every one in the whole world will become Islamic!

In the meaning of the word "Muslim"—one who submits to God—every one in the whole world will become Muslim!

In the meaning of the word "Krishna"—God consciousness—every one in the whole world will become Hindu!

In the meaning of the word "Messiah"—God's anointed one—every one in the whole world will become Jewish—Messianic!

In the meaning of the word "Atonement"—at-one-ment— Every one in the **Whole Universe** will become one with God and live in oneness with all created beings!

Please note that I did not say that every one will become "a Buddhist," "a Christian," "a Muslim," etc. But, *in the meaning of the word*, every one will become "Buddhist," "Christian," "Muslim,".... The Apostle Paul said that the whole creation groans, as in labor pains, waiting for God through His Spirit to give new birth to all, since all will eventually believe (Romans 8:18-23). **For that universal glory of God we eagerly and patiently wait with excitement and great anticipation (8:24, 25)!**

Discussion Questions

1. Why is it significant that God is not just loving, but God is love? How, then, could God's love [agape] ever fail (I Cor. 13:8)?

2. Why is light an appropriate symbol for God? What is the speed of light? Does light ever age?

3. Why is light an appropriate symbol for believers? What does it mean to be children of light and the light of the world?

4. Since God is spirit, what does it mean to be made in the image of God? What did Jesus mean by saying God seeks those who will worship in spirit and truth (John 4:24)?

5. Do you believe that all spirits came from God and that all spirits will return to God? Why or why not?

6. Does Christian Universalism honor and exalt Jesus' Holy name? Why or why not?

7. What implication does universal salvation, in all major religions, have for world peace? Why?

8. What do you understand by the concept of every one becoming "Buddhist," "Christian," "Hindu," Muslim," etc.?

Chapter 4
Integrity of Christians

The first "I" in the acrostic "CHRISTIANITY" represents "Integrity of Christians." Sadly, based on scientific-polling research, those who identify themselves as Fundamental and Evangelical Christians are not perceived by the general population in America to have much integrity. Even though people like Jesus, they do not like and do not want anything to do with the kind of Christianity these Christians represent.

In 2007, Gabe Lyons engaged David Kinnaman's research organization, the Barna Group, to do scientific research on the attitudes of the American public on Christians and Christianity. Based on the findings, they wrote the book, *unChristian.*[1] The picture is not a pretty one. What causes so many people, especially young people, to perceive Christians in such negative ways?

A Huge Image Problem

Kinnaman stated in the first chapter that Christianity has an image problem, and if it is not addressed, the church will fail to connect with a new generation. He said, "We are not responsible for outsiders' decisions, but we are accountable when our actions and attitudes—misrepresenting a holy, just, and loving God—have pushed outsiders away. Often Christianity's negative image reflects real problems, issues that Christians need to own and be accountable to change. My purpose in writing this book is to pry open the hearts and minds of Christians, to prepare us to deal with a future where people will be increasingly hostile and skeptical toward us. A new generation is waiting for us to respond."[2]

This author also shared this perspective, "One outsider from Mississippi made this blunt observation: 'Christianity has become bloated with blind followers who would rather repeat slogans than actually feel true compassion and care. Christianity has become marketed and streamlined into a juggernaut of fear mongering that has lost its own heart.'" This book does not mince words. "To engage non-Christians and point them to Jesus, we have to understand and approach them based on what they really think, not what we assume about them. We can't overcome their hostility by ignoring it. We need to understand their unvarnished views of us. Therefore, this book reflects outsiders' unfiltered reactions to Christianity"[3]

In addition, Kinnaman shared his aspirations for the future of the Christian Church. "I hope you will be challenged and inspired through the research and the contributors' thoughts. The church desperately needs more people to facilitate a deeper, more authentic vision of the Christian faith in our pluralistic, sophisticated culture."   The orientation of *unChristian* is clearly stated. "The main group we studied is "outsiders," those looking at the Christian faith from the outside. This group includes atheists, agnostics, those affiliated with a faith other than Christianity (such as Islam, Hinduism, Judaism, Mormonism, and so on), and other unchurched adults who are not born-again Christians. According to the research, part of the problem is we describe these people with derogatory labels and terms, which they often find offensive. Christians use terms like 'pagans' or 'the lost' or worse [heathen]. Other phrases are also inadequate, such as 'nonChristians' (which defines them simply by what they are not) as well as 'nonbelievers' or 'seekers' (labels that are not necessarily true of all outsiders)."[4]

Furthermore, *unChristian* insightfully addresses the problem of using labels. "Labeling people can undermine our ability to see them as human beings and as individuals…God wants us to pay attention to outsiders because he cares about them. *The Bible* says he patiently gives everyone time to turn to him (see 2 Peter 3:9)." In addition, "Christianity's image problem is not merely the perception of young outsiders. Those inside the church see it as well—especially Christians in their twenties and thirties."[5]

"Finally, this book is designed to be a mirror for you to see yourself and your faith reflected more clearly.   Through this process, God rolled up the blinds so I could see my own capacity for spiritual pride and how often self-absorption inhibits my ability to see people for who and what they really are. My prayer is that God will reveal your attitudes and stereotypes as you ponder this research. I hope you will more carefully consider how firmly people reject—and feel rejected by—Christians, and that you come away feeling inspired with ways you can make a difference."[6]

The research reported in *unChristian*, of outsiders' perception of evangelicals was "extraordinarily negative." Only three percent had a positive impression of evangelicalism. Thus, only about half a million out of 24 million have a favorable impression of evangelicals. This would apply to Fundamentalists as well. There is reported increasing hostility to conservative Christians in that those outside the church are responding in kind to the treatment they have experienced at the hands of "born-againers." An outsider had this to say, "Most people I meet assume that *Christian* means very conservative, entrenched in their thinking, antigay, antichoice, angry, violent, illogical, empire builders; they want to convert everyone, and they generally cannot live peacefully with anyone who doesn't believe what they believe." One might ask, why so negative? The answer is that Christians are often perceived for what they are against. *"We have become famous for what we oppose, rather than who we are for."*[7]

Most Common Perceptions

National surveys in the USA found these common perceptions of present-day Christianity among young people: anti-homosexual (91%), judgmental (87%), and hypocritical (85%)—the big-three negative impressions. Yes, there are other opinions held by the majority of adults in America: old-fashioned, too involved in politics, out of touch with reality, insensitive to others, boring, not accepting of other faiths, and confusing. "We are known for having an us-versus-them mentality...They feel minimized—or worse, demonized—by those who love Jesus...*This is what a new generation really thinks about Christianity.*"[8]

59

As reported on the same page, **"The most common 'favorable' impression is that Christianity teaches the same basic idea as other religions; more than four out of every five young outsiders embrace this description...Only a small percentage of outsiders strongly believe that the labels 'respect, love, hope, and trust' describe Christianity. A minority of outsiders perceives Christianity as genuine and real, as something that makes sense, and as relevant to their life." A huge problem of negative perception is that most outsiders understand almost all Christians believe Christianity claims to have a monopoly on salvation** [bold mine]!

Even worse, depending on whom you ask, not all professing Christians are going to heaven. The Roman Catholic Church claims to be the one true Christian Church. The same claim is made by the Eastern Orthodox Church as well as some very conservative Protestant Churches. Such exclusivity is offensive to other Christians and to adherents of other religious faiths.

Amazing Insight: Not What Christ Intended

"Like a corrupted computer file or a bad photocopy, Christianity, they say, is no longer in pure form, and so they reject it. One-quarter of outsiders say that their foremost perception of Christianity is off track and is not what Christ intended. *Modern-day Christianity no longer seems Christian*" [bold mine].[9] THIS IS TRULY AMAZING INSIGHT! Without knowledge of theology or church history, young people appear to have an innate understanding of what genuine Christianity should be like. They are right; this is not the Christianity taught by Jesus, preached by the apostles, and believed by the early church for over 500 years until it was corrupted by becoming the state church of the Roman Empire. God has written the truth on human hearts!

Religious Hijacking of Jesus

Those who desire to share their Christian faith should do as Kinnaman and Lyons contend: that is, to connect with people with a life-changing Jesus rather than an unChristian version of Him. They used a descriptive term—"Hijacking Jesus." "As we work to change the negative perceptions of outsiders, we need to avoid an opposite and equally dangerous extreme. Some Christians respond to outsiders' negativity by promoting a less offensive faith. They hijack the image of Jesus by portraying him as an open-minded, big-hearted, and never-offended-anyone moral teacher. That is an entirely wrong idea of Jesus. He taught remarkably tough truths about human beings and about sin." They stated, "Jesus' second coming will be equal parts glorious and dangerous...."[10]

Here, it seems, these authors' conservative theology has gotten in the way of doing what they are trying to do in the writing of unChristian. What they contend Christians must not do is exactly what those who want to present a positive image of Jesus must do in order to rescue Jesus' image from the religious hijackers.

True, Jesus did teach tough truths about human behavior and sin, but He never condemned a confessed sinner. As I pointed out in *Spiritual Terrorism*, the only people Jesus ever condemned were unrepentant, self-righteous religious officials who were oppressing the common people with legalism. These authors stated the case for how Jesus related to all kinds of people, especially confessed sinners. "Jesus was called a friend of sinners, relentlessly pursuing the downtrodden. What an irony that today his followers are seen in the opposite light!" **They also reported that many outside the church [and some in it] seldom see, "Christians who embody service, compassion, humility, forgiveness, patience, kindness, peace, joy, goodness, and love"** [bold mine].[11]

A Biblical Worldview

Kinnaman and Lyons have a section toward the end of their book, The Research: Key Terms Used. One such term is "Biblical worldview—a life perspective that enables a person to understand and respond to reality in light of what *the Bible* teaches." In its surveys, the Barna team defines a biblical worldview on the basis of several questions about religious beliefs. The definition requires someone to believe that unchanging moral truth exists; the source of moral truth is *the Bible*; *the Bible* is accurate in all of the principles it teaches; that eternal spiritual salvation cannot be earned; Jesus lived a sinless life on earth; every person has a responsibility to share religious beliefs with others; Satan is a living force, not just a symbol of evil; and God is the all-knowing, all-powerful maker of the universe who still rules His creation.[12]

Another word used in this section on "The Research," is "Outsiders—those individuals who look at Christianity from the outside in. This group includes atheists and agnostics; those affiliated with a faith other than Christianity (such as Islam, Hinduism, Judaism, Mormonism, and so on), and other unchurched adults who are not born again Christians."[13]

Did you notice in listing non-Christian religions that Kinnaman and Lyons also listed "Mormonism"? This is a problem of "judgmentalism" in the Republican primaries in 2012. According to polling, many Evangelical Christians have not and will not vote for a Mormon, which is the faith of candidate Mitt Romney. As the Republican candidate for president, he may well lose the election not just for his perceived "flip flopping" on various issues but due to his Mormon faith [some Evangelicals just not voting].

I have talked with a good number of Mormons, and they claim to have a Biblical worldview. When they witness to me, I share my Trinitarian belief in Christ and Christian Universalism with them. They have some different beliefs from most Christians, to be sure, but they claim Biblical authority, since they believe *the Bible* and contend the *Book of Mormon* is not in contradiction to *the Bible*. Such a practice is baptizing for the dead for which their church, "The Church of Jesus Christ of Latter Day Saints (LDS)," has come under criticism in 2012 for baptizing deceased Jews as well as other non-Mormons. But they claim Biblical authority for this practice based on I Corinthians 15:29.

The LDS actually has a more loving view of God than most Christians do. In regard to eternal punishment in hell, Mormons believe, unlike most Christians, that God will give sinners a second chance, and then, if they do not accept Christ, God will burn them in hell forever. They claim to be Christians, and since I do what Jesus said to do—not judge—I accept their word for their faith.

I definitely have a Biblical worldview; I believe that *the Bible* is true, but the Bible is certainly not the sole source of spiritual truth. As I have presented in *Spiritual Terrorism* and in this book, other religions have good moral values. The other religions listed as non-Christian do not claim to be Christian while the Mormon faith does. There may be misunderstanding about the term "born-again" Christians. This research also listed outsiders as the unchurched who are not born again. I have had hospice patients tell me that they are Christians, but they are not born again. Those who are "born-again" believers claim that they are the only true Christians; no one else is going to heaven. Thus, "born again" is a negative term for many.

The book u*nChristian* is well researched and written. I have quoted only a very small part of it. I strongly recommend it and urge all Christians to read it, study it, take the findings seriously, and change behavior which will change negative perceptions of Christians. It should be studied in Sunday school classes for teens and adults and be used as the format for home Bible studies.

An Excellent Follow-Up Book

In 2010 Gabe Lyons wrote a follow-up book on the current religious scene in The United States of America, *The Next Christians: The Good News About the End of Christian America.* Lyons is an Evangelical Christian whose credentials are unquestionable. He is a graduate of Liberty University, the conservative-Christian institution of higher education founded by the late Dr. Jerry Falwell. Chapter 1 is revealingly titled, "A Fading Reality." Lyons shared his story, "Seven years ago, I was 27 years old and embarrassed to call myself *Christian*. This was especially odd because I was raised in a Christian home, graduated from a Christian college, and then served as vice president of a prominent Christian organization. By all accounts, I should have been one of Christianity's biggest fans."[14]

Lyons went on to say, "Unfortunately, I began to notice that the perceptions my friends and neighbors had about Christians were incredibly negative. In fact, their past experiences with anything labeled *Christian* had sent them running in the opposite direction. Ironically, I came to empathize with their views. Having grown up in a Christian bubble myself, I witnessed countless instances when the lives of Christ followers were incongruent with Jesus' call to be loving, engaged, sacrificial, unselfish, and compassionate contributors to culture. The angst these experiences created would scare anyone from taking a second look at Jesus."[15]

Another Graduate of Liberty University

A few months ago, a man from Florida emailed me to say that he was reared in a Fundamental Christian Church in which he was spiritually abused. Ironically, his loving father was the pastor. Jim told me that he graduated from Liberty University, which should tell me a lot about his Evangelical orientation, and it certainly does. He reported that he is about 50 years old and does not attend church at all, nor does he watch any religious programs on TV, since, in his words, "Ninety-nine percent of it turns my stomach!" He shared that, to his delight, he had discovered my website: HealingSpiritualTerrorism.com, and "It is so life giving!" Jim stated that he thoroughly enjoyed reading my book, "*Spiritual Terrorism*," and it is very enlightening. It exposes the spiritual abuse/terrorism he experienced. He wrote a five-star review of *Spiritual Terrorism* and posted it on Amazon.com, identifying himself as J.A. Kidd.

An Indictment of Present-Day Christianity

According to Gabe Lyons, he was deeply burdened about this trend concerning loss of Christian influence in our contemporary culture. Lyons made the decision to leave his current occupation to launch a nonprofit organization to research the perceptions that sixteen to twenty-nine-year olds have about Christians. Lyons stated that the study confirmed his worst fears about the negative perceptions he had experienced. An overwhelming percentage of non-Christians sampled said that they perceive Christians as judgmental, hypocritical, too political, and anti-homosexual, among other things. What this researcher authored in this book builds on what he reported in the earlier book he coauthored, *unChristian*.

Research shows that over 76% of Americans claim to be Christian, but many are not proud of that label. Lyons sees a new way forward. "There is a whole movement of Christians—Evangelicals, mainline Protestants, Orthodox, Pentecostals, and others—asking the same questions and offering meaningful answers. They want to be a **force for restoration in a broken world** [bold mine] even as we proclaim the Christian gospel. They want the label *Christian* to mean something good, intelligent, authentic, true, and beautiful."[16]

Lyons reported a conversation which he had with a Christian friend who is a successful businessman. This man stated that he does not call himself a Christian anymore. He follows Christ as faithfully as he can, but he doesn't want to be associated with what the word "Christian" and what that brand has come to represent in the world. What a horrible indictment of present-day Christianity!

The End of the World as We Know it

The above is the subheading in chapter two in which Lyons stated, "A perfect storm of change is brewing over America. It's impossible for me to overstate this reality. Christianity has experienced many makeovers in the past two thousand years....No cultural shift is an island unto itself, but rather it is intimately connected to the historical movement from which it arises. So it is with the demise of Christian America."[17]

In 2004, Newsweek did a special report on "Spirituality in America," which was the cover story. According to Lyons it was an impressive dose of irony. For the last decade or so, respected religious leaders had been lamenting the death of Christian values in America. And now, the mainstream media were heralding Americans' quest for God. Who was right? It seems they both were. Eighty percent of Americans considered themselves to be spiritual; 75 percent reported wanting to develop a personal connection with God, but just about a third attended church regularly. Yes, Americans are a spiritual people, but, according to Lyons, they have started seeking spiritual growth outside traditional religions. He contends that this shift is not all bad.[18]

Lyons expressed this truth beautifully and graphically. "What if it's not a category 5 typhoon of spiritual death? What if it's not the bleak trumpet of apocalypse? What if it's actually a harnessable wind that can refill the sails of our faith?...Most people are seeking truth. Americans may not be convinced that there is only one way to God, and they may be more skeptical toward Christianity than any other organized religion, but today they are compelled to experiment. They are open to new paths of spirituality; they are seeking approaches to faith that connect with the inner longings of their soul."[19] This is great insight! And I strongly recommend both of these books on the religious views; there is much more to learn.

This is a great question asked by Lyons, "Could the end of Christian America become the stirrings of something beautiful? Is it possible to call a ceasefire in the culture war and still win the world?...They recognize these longings aren't really all that new. They are actually quite old and completely human. In the midst of change, the promise of good news is palpable. For those attuned to it, enormous possibilities await."[20]

Indeed, great opportunities do await all of us who seek to grow spiritually, which cannot happen in an atmosphere of fear-based religion, including Christianity. In both *unChristian* and *The Next Generation*, the authors insightfully stated that many Christians want to be involved in the restoration of the world. This is exactly the work we are to be doing in the world today in the interval between Christ's Ascension and Second Advent.

According to *the Bible*, heaven must receive Christ until the time of UNIVERSAL restoration of which all the holy prophets spoke since the world began (Acts 3:21 NEW RSV), [bold and caps mine]. For Christians, the desired spiritual growth can take place in the context of love-based Christianity when they hear of Christian Universalism. CU reveals that all people are equal before God. God desires all to be saved, and ultimately all will, in fact, be saved! But what will it take to accomplish this?

The Rise of the "Nones"

Time Magazine annually does an issue on "The Top Ten Things that are Changing the World" or "Changing Your Life." The March 12, 2012, issue is titled, "10 Ideas that are Changing Your Life." Idea number four is, "The Rise of the Nones." On surveys asking respondents to designate their religious faith, these are the people who respond: "None of the above." These people are not anti-religious or nonreligious; they have been turned off and have dropped out of organized religion. Many are Christians, but they just can't believe in the kind of Christianity they have been taught. This is the kind of Christianity of which Kinnaman and Lyons reported in regard to their scientific polling on what the general population thinks of religion in America in the 21st Century.

According to *Time Magazine*, the "Nones" may worship and fellowship in small groups in homes, outdoors, or wherever they may meet. These are good people who love God and their neighbors and want to make this world a better place, not just wait for the next one in heaven. They are non-judgmental and not homophobic. In essence, they believe in "live and let live." Come to think of it, this is exactly the kind of spirituality Jesus taught!

This group of spiritual, not necessarily religious, believers is not going away, and they are growing and growing rapidly. In 1990 the "Nones" numbered less than eight million. In 2011 the "Nones" numbered 16 million. This is the third largest spiritual/religious group in the USA right behind the second-place Southern Baptists who numbered about 16.2 million and far ahead of the third-place

United Methodist Church with just a bit less than eight million members. The largest group is Roman Catholic members who numbered 68.5 million. In 2011 the Catholic Church reported membership up half a percent, which is a change from the loss in the last two decades of many members, due to the sexual abuse of children by pedophilic priests.

At the rate the "Nones" are growing, they may well double again in the next decade, which would put them at 32 million. Doubling again in the following decade would bring them close to the Catholic Church membership. That is, assuming the Catholic Church does not grow significantly or even declines which appears to be the long-term trend. There are many former Catholics numbered among the "Nones."

Matthew Fox, a former Roman Catholic priest who was ousted for being too ecumenical and is now an Episcopal priest, has written a prophetic book in which he foresees the eventual demise of the Catholic Church as it is presently constituted. He gave an example of a group of 150 people attending a seminar he was teaching on spirituality. He asked how many of those in the group had grown up in the Catholic Church, and 100 hands went up. He then asked how many of them had children who were practicing Catholics, and all 100 hands went down. Young people are turned off by the Christianity of most Churches, Catholic or Protestant, today! His book is *The Pope's War: Why Ratzinger's Secret Crusade Has Imperiled the Church and How it Can be Saved.*[21]

I wrote in *Spiritual Terrorism* that the Roman Catholic hierarchy would like for Catholics and the public to believe the scandals of priests who sexually abuse children is just the American media blowing things way out of proportion. Dr. Albert LaChance, who wrote the book, *The Modern Christian Mystic: Finding the Unitive Presence of God,*[22] told me by phone that this is a real problem in the Catholic Church and that he was sexually abused by a priest. Dr. LaChance twice interviewed me on his radio program, "God Talk." He related that he had attended Mass every day [not just every Sunday] for over 25 years. When the

Catholic Church ignored his allegations of abuse, he left the church and is now an Episcopal.

As I pointed out in *Spiritual Terrorism*, the sexual-abuse scandal is as bad or worse in Ireland, which is a stronghold of Catholicism. Fox shared the belief of many young people in Ireland that the Roman Catholic Church hierarchy is composed of old men who tolerate and facilitate the sexual abuse of children by covering it up. Needless to say, many young adults have dropped out of the Catholic Church. This global problem and awareness of the complicity of those in power in the church have caused millions of Catholics to turn off and drop out of church.

Fox believes, as I do, that eventually a newly restored catholic church will truly be universal in the meaning of the Latin word, "catholic." That catholic/universal church will, of course, teach the Good News of universal salvation, the message which Jesus taught and for which He died. This all-loving message of God's unconditional love for all people will resonate with these young adults who will restore the Christian Church. In *The Pope's War* Fox stated that the Christian Church can and will be saved from destruction from within by the universal church universally understanding God's universal love and universal salvation, living in the liberating power of it, and sharing it with the world.[23]

With this understanding of universal love firmly in mind, spirit-filled Christians, propelled by the grace, mercy, and unconditional love of God will join hands with members of other religions, also propelled by the same unconditional love, grace, and mercy to bring healing to our world torn by religious strife. Will you join the movement to break free from fear-based religion and change the world for the good of all?

TWO IDEAS WHICH ARE CHANGING THE WORLD

My book *Spiritual Terrorism* was published April 7, 2008. The manuscript had, of course, been submitted to the publisher well before the publication date. While waiting for the initial printing, I happened to read, in a doctor's office, *Time Magazine*, "10 Ideas that are changing the world," dated March 24, 2008. The 10 ideas covered the environment, the economy, technology, and religion. It was too late to include this source in my book, but I was glad to discover that two of the 10 ideas, stated in principle and concept, are in my book—Idea # 4, "Reverse Radicalism" of terrorists and idea # 10: "Re-Judaizing Jesus."

Idea # 4: According to *Time*, "Serious study of terrorism has, for the past 20 years, been fixated on one question. That question, so teasingly close to the right one, is, 'Why do people join terrorist groups?'...The smarter question, the experts have now begun to ask, is, 'Why do people *leave* terrorist groups?'" "Basically, they become disenchanted with the terrorist's lifestyle and reality that didn't live up to the fantasy. *Time* reported, "Nearly a dozen countries, including the U.S. [while in Iraq], have recently started programs to educate radicals about the gap between their religious ideals and the groups they follow...with the help of clerics and ex-terrorists. 'We've been fighting the wrong battle,' says Frank Cilluffo, a former White House Homeland Security official who is researching deradicalization at George Washington University.'"

As reported, this approach of using clergy with a very loving conception of God, to teach captured terrorists that Islam neither teaches nor condones the killing of innocent men, women, and children is working. *Time* said that data are scarce about the success of such programs. But Saudi Arabia has reported an eighty percent success rate in reversing radicalization of terrorists and converting them to law-abiding, peaceful, productive citizens. This approach is much more effective and far less costly than military action. *The power of God's love to change minds and lives is far greater than the power of fear!* **The greatest is love** (I Cor. 13:13)!

Idea # 10: "Re-Judaizing Jesus" means to understand not only that Jesus was a Jew but to interpret what he taught within the context of Judaism. *Time* insightfully reported that this is a "seismic" shift in that for centuries Christians have been interpreting the Hebrew Scriptures in the context of Gentile culture. "But today seminaries across the Christian spectrum teach, as Vanderbilt University New Testament scholar Amy Jill Levine says, that 'if you get the [Jewish] context wrong, you will certainly get Jesus wrong.'"

This concept of understanding what Jesus taught within the context of Judaism is especially important in regard to correctly interpreting "unquenchable fire" of hell which, when taken out of the context of Jewish culture, has been used to terrorize literal-minded Christians. Jesus used fire metaphorically, as did Moses, Isaiah, Zechariah, Malachi, and others to symbolize purification. Unquenchable fire is not, **as spiritual terrorists contend**, fire that will never go out; it is fire which will not be extinguished. But it will burn out when it has consumed the spiritually combustible material which is sin. Thus, when sin has been consumed, having purified sinners, the unquenchable fire will go out as all fires do.

The Torah (Old Testament) says that the Messiah will be like a refining fire to purify the Jews (Mal. 3:1-3). Believers will be purified by fire at the Judgment Seat of Christ (I Cor. 3:10-15). Unbelievers will be purified by fire [*The Good News Bible: Today's English Version*] in hell—according to Jesus' mixed metaphor—"salted with fire" (Mk. 9:49).

Eventually, ALL will be purified and reconciled to God as evidenced by universal submission and confession (Isaiah 45:23-25; 66:23; Rom. 14:9-11; Phil. 2:9-11)! Two universally recognized signs of submission are kneeling and prostration. Kneeling means to rest one's knees on the surface on which one was standing while prostration means to bend forward on the knees until one's forehead is touching the floor or ground. This symbolizes ultimate submission—head lower than the heart. Christians kneel as a sign of submission to Christ. Muslims prostrate themselves to signify total submission to God, since the word "Muslim" means one who submits to God, and the word "Islam" means submission to God. If we Christians are right about Jesus being God incarnate—God and Jesus being One—are not we and Muslims merely expressing submission to God differently?

71

Discussion Questions

1. Do you believe in the ongoing demise of "Christian" America?

2. Is this a bad or good thing—crisis or opportunity?

3. Would you describe yourself as a spiritual and/or religious person? Why or why not?

4. Do you believe that only Christians will go to heaven? On what do you base your belief?

5. Do you believe all people will come to believe in Jesus the Savior of the world?

6. What do the Holy Scriptures mean by the term, "universal restoration" in Acts 3:21 NRSV?

7. What is the potential for universal belief in universal salvation to heal the world?

8. Can we only have peace on earth due to Christ's Second Advent, with Him establishing His millennial reign (Rev. 20), or can we have peace before that (Isaiah 2:4)? Why or why not?

9. What do you think of the potential to prevent or reverse radicalization of terrorists with love-based religion?

10. What does the term "Re-Judaizing Jesus" mean? How may this process enrich our understanding of the Holy Scriptures?

Chapter 5
Symbolism of Fire

The "S" in the acrostic "CHRISTIANITY, represents "Symbolism of Fire." Symbolism in *The Holy Bible* is bountiful, beautiful, timeless, and cross cultural. Many words, therefore, are not literally true. Thus, fire is a very prominent and significant symbol in the sacred writings of Christianity and other religions.

One of the four Biblical definitions of The Supreme Being is "God is a consuming fire" (Deut. 4:24; Heb. 12:29). In religious literature, suffering and punishment in fire are symbolic of the spiritually corrective nature of metaphorical fire. A literal interpretation of the symbolism of fire is a major cause of fear, spiritual insanity, and spiritual abuse—especially spiritual terrorism, spiritual abuse in its most extreme form.

Tasker, General Editor of the Evangelical, *Tyndale New Testament Commentaries*, stated, in regard to "aeonian" in Mt. 25:46 having been mistranslated as "eternal," it would be "difficult to exaggerate" the harm that is done "…when 'fire' is understood in a literal rather than in a metaphorical sense."[1]

Judaism

The metaphorical use of fire is a significant feature of Judaism which includes sulfur and salt symbolism. The story of the destruction of the cities of Sodom and Gomorrah is an excellent case in point (Gen. 19:24-26).

Here we have in Genesis, written about 1,500 years before Christ, a preview of God's redemptive strategy. This is the whole metaphorical and allegorical picture. Literalists are so driven to prove that this story literally happened that they miss the big symbolic picture. In the previous chapter of Genesis, the Lord informed Abraham that he was going to destroy those two cities due to their wickedness. **For those who contend one must not question God, Abraham must have not gotten that message.**

Abraham asked two very profound philosophical and theological questions, **"Will you destroy the righteous with the wicked" (18:23)? And "Will not the Judge of all the earth do right" (18:25)?** The answers were that God would not destroy the righteous, and He would do right. The Lord thus sent two angels to Abraham's nephew, Lot, to warn him and save him and his family, since they were the only righteous ones in either city. The angels escorted Lot, his wife and daughters out of range of the fire and brimstone/sulfur and told them not to even look back. But his wife did look back and was turned into a pillar of salt.

What are the spiritual lessons to be learned? God gives ample warning to the righteous and does what is right. Lot and his daughters were saved by grace, the easy way through obedience. Lot's wife was turned into salt for disobedience. A question which reveals my analytical bent, I have asked many people, **"Why was Lot's wife turned into salt rather than into some other substance such as petrified wood, stone, bronze, iron, steel, etc.?"** Virtually all Christians know the story; most say the message is to obey God to the letter and never look back. I have yet for anyone to tell me that he or she has ever thought about why she was turned into salt rather than some other substance.

The answer is that salt is a preservative which preserves by purifying. The Law of Moses required salt to be offered with meat offerings. This was the salt of the Covenant made with fire symbolizing purification (Lev. 2:13-16). **Lot's wife was saved the hard way of being "salted" which is also a means of grace.**

The backdrop of this metaphorical drama was the wicked people of Sodom and Gomorrah being destroyed by burning sulfur for time, not eternity. Since burning sulfur symbolizes healing/purification, the wicked will be healed of their sins and eventually accepted into heaven. The ancients readily understood this metaphorical use of fire and sulfur—burning sulfur. Indeed, it is a shame that many modern people, especially conservative Christians, are so literal minded that they fail to grasp the truth in this beautiful, timeless, cross-cultural symbolic language.

Such symbolism is like international travel signs—no words are needed, just the visual image. To use a modern analogy, if *the Bible* would have said that, after The Final Judgment, all those infected with sin will be cast into a fiery lake of penicillin, would that not logically symbolize healing sin infection? Sulfur was the wonder drug in the ancient world as penicillin is today.

Isaiah uses fiery language to describe the fury of God toward sin. He comes **burning** with anger; His lips are full of indignation, and **His tongue is as a devouring fire. The breath of God is like a stream of burning sulfur** (30:27-33). Isaiah also declared that **the judgmental fire of God will be unquenchable** (66:24). It will, therefore, purify those who have rebelled against God and have been resisting His saving grace. The result will eventually be universal worship of the one living God as evidenced by every knee bowing and every tongue confessing faith in Him (45:21-25; 66:23). Zechariah (13:9) and Malachi (3:1-3) also describe the fiery judgment of God. Malachi closes with this commission. The people of the Covenant are told to go forth and tread down the wicked. The symbolism of the consuming fire is continued with assurance that the wicked shall be "ashes" under their feet (4:3).

Christianity

With the final-prophetic message of Malachi, there were 400 years in which no prophet of Israel was heard. This span of four centuries is known by Christians as, "The Intertestamental Period." Suddenly the long-prophetic silence was shattered by the cry of a baby—the Jewish Messiah who was born of the Blessed Virgin Mary. Jesus was Jewish in every sense. His parents were Jews, His culture was Jewish, and His religion was Judaism. He prophetically proclaimed to his people that the first commandment is, "Hear O Israel; The Lord our God is one Lord" (Mark 12:29). This, of course, is a quotation from the Law of Moses (Deut. 6:4).

Jesus acted totally within the Jewish tradition of great prophets by castigating the people for their sin of failing to live up to their calling as the people of the Covenant. He, like all Jewish prophets of *The Torah* before him, called the covenantal people to a higher standard. He also continued the metaphorical use of fire.

John the Baptist was in that same-great Jewish-prophetic tradition in the symbolic use of fire. Referring to the people of the Covenant and calling them to be faithful and fruitful, he declared to them, just prior to his baptism of Jesus, that the Messiah would baptize with the Holy Spirit and with fire, and there would be a judgment of unquenchable fire (Mt. 3:10-12).

We can say three things with certainty about Jesus' use of the word "fire." He used fire in a metaphorical—not a literal sense. He used it not to instill a morbid fear of God in the people of the Covenant but to convey the purifying message of God as the consuming fire in order to call them to a higher standard. Jesus used fire in the same sense as Moses, Isaiah, Zechariah, Malachi, John the Baptist, as well as other Jewish prophets.

Not one used fire in a literal or negative sense, which must be kept in mind as one reads Jesus' words in regard to hell fire that may appear to teach eternal punishment. A good example of that is Jesus' teaching about the unrighteous being consigned to the "aeonian" fire prepared for the devil and his angels (Mt. 25:41).

Jesus validated the Jewish prophets' metaphorical use of fire when he stated that the fire of hell will not be quenched (Mark 9:48). Unquenchable does not mean that the fire will never go out, only that it will not be put out or extinguished. But it will burn out when it has accomplished the purifying purpose for which God created it. Jesus left absolutely no doubt about His symbolic use of fire when He stated the purpose of hell, "For every one shall be salted with fire, and every sacrifice shall be salted with salt" (Mark 9:49). In the Aramaic which Jesus spoke, speakers expressed themselves in the strongest words possible to make their point. Thus, Jesus used strong though not literal-meaning words.

Mild Accuracy Weakness

Dr. Rocco Errico, a scholar in Aramaic, said in *And There Was Light* that an Aramaic speaker's purpose was not to deliver the message in scientifically accurate terms. "He piles up his metaphors and superlatives, reinforced by a theatrical display of gestures and facial expression in order to make the hearer feel his meaning. He speaks as it were in pictures...It is also because he loves to speak in pictures and to subordinate literal accuracy to the total impression of an utterance, that he makes such extensive use of figurative language...he is fond of metaphor, exaggeration, and positiveness in speech. To him mild accuracy is weakness."[2]

This understanding of the Aramaic language and culture explains exactly why Jesus used all these strong picture words in general and, especially in regard to hell—weeping, wailing, gnashing of teeth, cutting off one's hands and feet and gouging out one's eyes, unquenchable fire, being salted with fire, etc., because He needed to communicate in the manner His audience would have readily understood. **They would not have taken such word pictures literally. On the other hand, they would have considered mild accuracy weakness!** If Jesus had spoken in a mild manner, He may have lost his audience as they became bored and walked away. Even if they had not walked away, they may have missed His point if He were speaking in a style unfamiliar to them.

When trying to correct the inconsistency between what the Pharisees taught and what they did, Jesus could have said in our Western-world abstract style, "Your teachings and your behavior are incongruent." But Jesus, as an excellent Aramaic speaker, exclaimed, "blind guides," "child of hell," "fools," "hypocrites," "serpents and generation of vipers," "strain out a gnat and swallow a camel," "whitewashed tombs" [clean on the outside but a stench on the inside], and "How can you escape the damnation of hell" (Mt. 23:13-33)?

Doubtlessly, Jesus deliberately mixed the metaphors of fire and salt to make it impossible for literalists to logically interpret this metaphorical language literally. It is, of course, IMPOSSIBLE to **literally** salt anyone or anything with fire. And yet literalists, locked into a mindset of literalism, still interpret Jesus' words literally. This is a major cause of spiritual abuse/terrorism and spiritual insanity. **Some victims of spiritual insanity become spiritually and mentally insane and homicidal and/or suicidal!**

Christian Conceptions of Hell
Extremely Abusive

1. Hell is worse than literal fire for eternal torture of sinners. This is the view of Bill Wiese in his book, *23 Minutes in Hell* and Robert Morey in his book, *Death and the Afterlife*.

2. Hell is literal fire for eternal torture of sinners. This is the view of Fundamental and many Evangelical Christians.

Moderately Abusive

3. Hell is not literal fire but symbolizes a torturous existence of sinners in it. This is the view of some Evangelical and most mainline Protestant Christians [if they believe in hell].

4. Hell fire is for the purpose of annihilating sinners so they will cease to exist. The annihilation may be instant or progressive, but no one will be tormented forever. This is the view of the late Drs. Clark Pinnock and John Stott.

Mildly Abusive

5. Hell symbolizes nonexistence, but God will not annihilate sinners. They will go to "sleep" at death and never awaken. This view is called "Conditional Immortality." God will bestow immortality on those who accept Christ as Savior.

6. Hell fire symbolizes purification of sinners. But sinners will not be saved due to them forever saying "No" to God's offer of salvation and God not violating their free will. This is the view of Rob Bell in his best-selling book, *Love Wins:*

A Book About Heaven, Hell, and the Fate of Every Person Who Has Ever Lived [whose fate Bell laves uncertain].

7. Hell fire is for purification, and almost all sinners will be saved. But not all will be saved, because after God, as fire, has consumed all the sin in some people there will be nothing good in them, so the fire that consumes sin will then consume such sinners. This is the view of Sharon Baker in her book, *Razing Hell: Rethinking Everything You've Been Taught About God's Wrath and Judgment.*

Non-Abusive

8. Hell fire symbolizes purification of sinners. And, eventually, without coercing or violating free will, all sinners will say, "Yes" to God's offer of salvation and be saved. Theoretically, in this view, sinners in hell could say "No" to God's offer of salvation forever, since God will never violate free will. It is certain that they will not say "No" forever as evidenced by Christ drawing all to Himself (John 12:32), universal submission and confession of faith in Christ (Phil. 2:9-11), all living in Christ and God being all in all (I Cor. 15:22, 28), and universal worship (Rev. 5:13). This is my view and that of these authors who believe in Christian Universalism: Gerry Beauchemin in, *Hope Beyond Hell: The Righteous Purpose of God's Judgment*; Bob Evely in, *At the End of the Ages: The Abolition of Hell*; Kalen Fristad in, *Destined For Salvation: God's Promise to Save Everyone*; Eric Stetson in, *Christian Universalism: Good News For All People*; and Thomas Talbott in, *The Inescapable Love of God.*

9. Other Christian Universalists believe that there is no hell except life on earth being hell. Bell made a good case for this view in *Love Wins* though this is not his stated position. It is the view expressed by Allan Chevrier in, *Whatever Became of Melanie?* Julie Ferwerda in, *Raising Hell: Christianity's Most Controversial Doctrine Put Under Fire;* and Michael Riley and James William in, *Is God*

Fair? What About Gandhi? and Gary Amirault at Tentmaker. org. This no-hell view is generally called "Ultra-Universalism."

With all of these views of hell, and perhaps variations of these, among those who believe *the Bible* is the Word of God, can not we Christians just agree to disagree agreeably on the issue of hell? Mature faith will trust God to do the right, not the wrong, thing.

Christian Universalism in Hymns

There are some great hymns of the Christian faith that are accurate statements of Biblical truth including the truth of Christian Universalism. The hymn, "Guide Me, O Thou Great Jehovah," is right on point about the death of death itself by Christ's resurrection from the dead (I Cor. 15:54-57) and the eventual destruction of hell itself, according to Jesus (Mt. 16:18). "...Bid my anxious fears subside; **death of death and hell's destruction,** land me safe on Canaan's side [an allusion to heaven].... Another great hymn is, "God Leads His Dear Children Along." Key words are, "Some through the water, some through the flood, **some through the fire**, but all through the blood."

Islam

There are many usages of the word "fire" in regard to hell in the *Holy Koran.* Some passages do not sound so bad while some sound really awful. For example, "And fear the Fire, which is prepared for those who reject Faith (3:131). Soon shall We cast terror into the hearts of the unbelievers...their abode will be the Fire (3:151)! They (Satan's dupes) will have their dwelling in hell, and from it they will find no escape (4:121).

Some verses in the *Koran* seem to indicate that the fire of hell may be for purification—"chastisement"—while other verses sound like hell is forever. "No escape," however, from hell is not necessarily the same thing as no release. Prisoners may not be able to escape from prison, but all except "lifers" are eventually released when they have served their sentences.

Muslim literalists interpreting "no escape" in the *Koran* as meaning eternal punishment may be like Christian literalists interpreting "unquenchable fire" as burning forever when, obviously, the fire will go out when it has consumed the spiritually combustible material—sin. The Sufi scholars, mystics, and poets, as well as lay people, interpret the fire of hell metaphorically; therefore, they believe that the fire symbolizes purification in which case, eventually, all will be cleansed of their sins and reconciled to God, our heavenly Father.

Sufism, apparently, is accepted as a valid, historical branch of mainstream Islam, but literalists reject their interpretation of *the Holy Koran* as heresy. I mentioned previously that Saudi Arabia has banned the teaching of Sufism in that country while permitting only the teaching of Wahabaism. Muslims who believe in Wahabaism are Fundamentalists who, naturally, interpret the *Koran* literally. They have been polluting the minds of Saudis, in the mosques and in the schools, with literalism and the false doctrine of eternal punishment, since the Saudi royal family gained control of that country almost a century ago.

Since the Saudis have been thus spiritually abused with spiritual insanity, some of them have become political terrorists who are motivated by spiritual terrorism to carry out terroristic acts.. As the old saying goes, "The chickens have come home to roost." Osama Bin Laden was a product of this fundamental brand of Islam. It is no wonder that 15 of the 19 plane hijackers on September 11, 2001, were from Saudi Arabia. But Saudi Arabia is in as much danger from Al Qaeda as is the United States.

There have been various bombings in Saudi Arabia that have killed Muslims whom Al Qaeda believes are heretics. Of course, many innocent Muslims have been murdered as "collateral damage." The ruling royal family, whom Bin Laden wanted to overthrow in order to set up an Islamic Republic, has banned Al Qaeda from Saudi Arabia, but terrorist cells continue to operate.

Very importantly, the spiritually abusive system which produced these political terrorists has remained, but slowly that system is changing. Realizing the source of the problem, the royal family has sanctioned the teaching of a more loving version of Islam. It was announced by various TV and radio media in August of 2007 that Saudi Arabia has instituted a re-education program for Saudis who have been captured for terrorist activities.

A website which details this program is: "Postcard: Saudi Arabia—Time." The reporter, Scott Macleod, explained that the terrorists are given the option of regular prison or this spiritual rehabilitation program. The only requirement is that participants must be willing to consider changing their religious and political views. Only about 20 percent—the hardcore—refuse.

This rehabilitation program employs Islamic clergy, scholars, psychiatrists, and sociologists to teach that Allah is a God of Love, and *the Holy Koran* does not sanction the killing of fellow Muslims or innocent people of any faith. It will be interesting to see if the government lifts the ban on Sufism, which is the most loving form of Islam. People understanding God's unconditional love, grace, and mercy will take away the mind control by secular and religious authorities and will promote more loving behavior.

As reported, this re-education program is having a success rate of 80 percent in changing the minds and the behavior of young Muslim terrorists. They are returning to society as responsible citizens, being gainfully employed, getting married, and having families. Such a spiritual re-education program might work well in other religions as well, including Christianity. Would-be assassins of doctors who perform abortions, terrorists who would bomb abortion clinics killing innocent people in the process, and terrorists who would bomb federal buildings or other facilities, killing innocent men, women, and children in their zeal for God might be deterred by such a program.

No, I am not suggesting a government-mandated re-education program. Since we have freedom of religion, speech, press, etc., unlike Saudi Arabia, I am advocating that people use their freedom to read [books portraying a totally positive image of God], think, study, and grow spiritually so that every one can be spiritually as well as legally free. According to Jesus, truth frees (John 8:32)!

Eastern Religions

In five thousand years of the history of Hinduism, the oldest religion with no known founder, Agni was the god of fire as seen in flame, lightning, and the sun. "Agni" is the word for fire in the Sanskrit, the ancient Indo-European language, which is the mother tongue of various modern-European languages and those on the subcontinent of India. Much like the sacrificial system in Judaism in which fire consumed the sacrifices on the altar, Agni consumed the offerings in Hinduism. Over 200 of more than 1,000 songs in the Rig Veda, a collection of Hindu hymns, are sung to Agni.

In polytheism (many gods), Hindus worshiped the god of fire, but over the millennia the aspect of fire evolved into an attribute of Brahman—the Hindu word for the One Supreme Being. In one of Christianity's definitions of God, "God is a consuming fire," fire is an attribute of God just as is light, love, and spirit. Though Hindus no longer worship the god of fire, the ritual of fire is a sacred part of Hinduism. It is celebrated at major life events such as births, weddings, and funerals, as well as major religious holidays. The saffron flag, a red-yellow color, is a symbol of fire in Buddhism, Sikhism, and Jainism as well as Hinduism. The symbolism of fire plays an important role in the home-fire ritual in Buddhism.

Other Religions

Zoroastrians, who worship before an altar of fire, have been accused of worshiping fire. This is not true; they do not worship fire. They worship God who is symbolized by the fire. Native Americans keep "sacred fires" burning. In the medicine wheel the sacred fire is pictured in the hub—the center of life.

The flame is a symbol of eternity in various religions and secular organizations. An "eternal flame" has burned continuously at a Buddhist temple in Japan for the last 1,200 years. An "eternal flame" burns at The Hague, in the Netherlands, at the Peace Palace symbolizing world peace. One also burns in Japan at the Hiroshima Peace Memorial, and it is to burn until all nuclear weapons have been abolished. **God, as fire, shall consume the sin in all humanity, and the fire of righteousness shall burn in the heart of every person until all are at one with God and are living in peace with one another!**

SMARTER THAN A PRESCHOOLER?

There is a popular TV Show, "Are You Smarter than a 5th Grader?" My question for adults, who believe in and live in fear of literal hell fire for themselves and/or loved ones, is "Are you smarter than a preschooler?" My three-year-old grandson pointed to the cover of my book, which is a picture of fire, and said, "Oh, fire!" He knew that fire will burn and hurt, so he knew not to touch hot things. I said, "Honey, this is not real fire. It is Biblical fire, which symbolizes purification, so it will not burn and hurt you." I knew that I had only a two-minute teachable moment to share spiritual truth with him in a way he could understand.

When he gets dirty, he likes to have a bath to get clean. I explained purification by fire as God's way of cleaning adults who get "dirty" with sin, and that hell is God's "timeout" for adults who sin by hurting others. It is like the Christian hymn, *How Firm a Foundation*, **"...The flame shall not hurt thee; I [God] only design thy dross to consume, and thy gold to refine."** Fire symbolizes purification in all major religions and some minor ones.

A few weeks after his fourth birthday, I was putting together a fire pit. My grandson, as always, wanted to help. After a few minutes, appearing to be in deep thought, he went into the house.

A couple of minutes later he returned holding my book. He pointed to the cover and said, "Biblical fire will not burn and hurt you." He then pointed to the picture of the blazing fire on the front of the box, in which the fire pit had come, and said, "That fire will burn and hurt you." I thought, "Wow, how smart and insightful!"

At only three years of age he had not only understood what I had shared with him, **in a two-minute "teachable moment,"** but, at only four, demonstrated that he understood the difference between literal and symbolic fire. He understands what millions of literal-minded adult Christians, living in fear of hell fire which they believe to be literal and eternal, do not understand!

I shared this with my daughter and son-in-law, and they will reinforce his understanding, so that he will grow up to have reverence for God and a sense of awe (the meaning of Biblical "fear") about God with zero morbid fear of God. This will result in love and worship of God and service for God. What a contrast with the answer I received from a literalist preacher when, as a youngster, I specifically asked, "Could the fire of hell be a different kind of fire?" The response terrorized me, "*The Bible* says 'fire' and I believe it means 'fire!'" Not believing in literal fire meant not believing *the Bible*, not being a Christian, and, therefore, being condemned by God at death to literal hell fire forever!

This grandson is now seven years old—only a year younger than when my many-years-long nightmare of spiritual terrorism began. After overhearing some Christians say that hell fire is literal, my grandson said to my daughter, "Grandpa told me that Biblical fire will not burn and hurt me. Is that right? She said, "Yes, honey, Biblical fire symbolizes correction." I am so thankful he will not be spiritually terrorized as I was.

Millions of Christian parents lovingly guard their children against pornographic Internet sites, violence on TV, scary movies, etc., but they, with the best of intentions, take their children to churches which expose them to spiritually abusive preaching and teaching about God torturing "unsaved" children, as well as adults, in hell fire forever! Teaching children that hell is literal/eternal fire is **CHILD ABUSE—SPIRITUAL PORNOGRAPHY!**

Children must be able to perceive God to be at least as loving as their loving parents in order to develop a spiritually healthy conception of God. Otherwise, though they may well grow up to believe in God, they will never be able to trust God! STOP ALL FORMS OF CHILD ABUSE INCLUDING SPIRITUAL ABUSE!

Victims of spiritual terrorism, due to spiritual insanity, from across the country and around the world, have been healed by reading *Spiritual Terrorism*. Adults healed of spiritual insanity, children prevented from being spiritually terrorized, fear being cast out and people perfected in God's perfect love (I John 4:18) will optimize spiritual maturity and mental health. <u>Universal understanding of purifying fire will have a greater impact on the world than the discovery of fire, resulting in universal peace (Isaiah 2:4)!</u>

Discussion Questions

1. Do you believe *the Bible* uses fire literally in relation to judgment and hell? Is it worse than literal fire? Why?
2. What about the Messiah's refining fire (Mal. 3:1-3)? Does the Messiah purifying Jews with symbolic fire make sense?
3. What about the Judgment Seat of Christ (I Cor. 3:10-15 and II Cor. 5:10))? Are the gold, silver, and precious stones and the wood, hay, and straw literal? If not, what does each symbolize? Is salvation an issue in these verses [v. 15]?
4. What does "God is a consuming fire" (Deut. 4:24; Heb. 12:29); breath of God like a stream of fire and brimstone—burning sulfur (Isa. 30:33) mean? How is the word of God like fire (Jer. 23:29)? At the burning bush, Moses was told to take off his shoes. (Ex. 3:1-5). Why? Holy ground; how?
5. What will God, as a consuming fire, consume: sin and sinners [annihilation]; neither sin nor sinners [eternal torture]; sin which will purify sinners [CU]? Which one(s) of these three options make(s) sense to you? Does one make perfect sense? If so, which one? Why?

Chapter 6
Total Love of God

The first "T" in the acrostic "CHRISTIANITY" represents "Total Love of God." This is the theological chapter in this book. Many Christians do not understand theology, find it boring, and are thus not interested in learning about it. However, every believer's life is affected by theology even though he or she may not be aware of the theological basis of one's faith. If not interested in theology, you may want to skip this chapter [perhaps read and study it later].

The Greek word for God is "Theos," so theology is the study of God. What people believe about God, in the final analysis, determines what they believe about Christ, heaven, hell, salvation, the nature of mankind, holy angels, fallen angels [including Satan], and other doctrines of the Christian faith.

The Universal Effectual Atonement

The word "universal" means that Christ died for everyone in general and the word "effectual" means that Christ died for each and every person in particular. The word "effectual" also means that each and every person for whom Christ died will ultimately be saved. Thus, since He died for all, all will eventually be saved. When, on the cross, Christ cried out, "It is finished," and died, He meant that God's plan of salvation was completed for every created being in the whole universe including the fallen angels. The universal scope of Christ's redemptive work is clearly expressed in the Holy Scriptures.

John the Baptist saw Jesus coming to him, and he exclaimed, "Behold, the Lamb of God who takes away the sin [singular, collective sin] of the world" (John 1:29). Jesus dealt with the collective "sin" of the world on the cross. Individual sins must be confessed but are also in the atonement. The best-known verse in *the Bible* is John 3:16, "For God so loved the world, that he gave his only begotten Son, that whosoever believeth in him should not perish, but have everlasting life." God loves the world in general and each and every person in particular!

The universality of Christ's atonement is expressed in I John 2:2 and 4:14. "And he is the propitiation [atoning sacrifice] for our sins: and not for ours only [present believers] but also for the sins [individual sins of all] of the whole world....And we have seen and do testify that the Father sent the Son to be the Savior of the world." The Book of Timothy teaches the same universal message that God desires all people to be saved and come to the knowledge of the truth (I Tim. 2:3-6). In Timothy, Paul also declared that our hope is set on the living God who is the Savior of all people (I Tim. 4:10). The Apostle Paul penned this glorious truth that we joy in God, through our Lord Jesus Christ, by whom we have received the atonement (Rom. 5:11 KJV).

In the Universal Effectual Atonement, God's love is truly unconditional and everlasting. This atonement of Christ declares exactly what *the Bible* says. For example, Psalm 136 is composed of 26 verses and in every verse it declares that God's mercy [KJV] (or love or steadfast love) is everlasting or endures forever! The prophet Jeremiah wrote, "The Lord hath appeared of old unto me, saying, 'Yea, I have loved thee with an everlasting love: therefore with lovingkindness have I drawn thee'" (31:3 KJV).

The ever-loving, blessed Holy Trinity truly acts in perfect harmony: God, the Father, created all people; God, the Son, died for all people; and God, the Holy Spirit, seeks the salvation of all people with saving grace which ultimately proves to be irresistible. All people will, therefore, be saved!

The great hymn writer, Fanny Crosby (1820-1915), got it right in her wonderful song, "To God Be the Glory." "To God be the glory, great things He hath done, so loved He the world that He gave us His Son, Who yielded His life an atonement for sin, and opened the life-gate so **all** may go in. Praise the Lord, praise the Lord, let the earth hear His voice! Praise the Lord, praise the Lord, let the people rejoice! O come to the Father thro' Jesus the Son, and give Him the glory; great things He hath done."

Maltbie Babcock (1858-1901) got it right as well in his great hymn, "This Is My Father's World." "This is my Father's world, O let me ne'er forget that though the wrong seems oft so strong, God is the Ruler yet. This is my Father's world: The battle is not done; **Jesus who died shall be satisfied, and earth and heaven be one."** Another version of the last line of this hymn is: "The Lord is King: let the heavens ring! God reigns: let earth be glad!"

We Christians pray in our Lord's Prayer, **"Thy kingdom come, Thy will be done on earth as it is in heaven…."** Jesus will never be satisfied until all for whom He died are saved and earth and heaven are, indeed, one. **Some glorious day, God's will shall be done on earth, in heaven, and throughout the universe! Christ will be satisfied, and every created being shall be glad!**

What more needs to be said or could possibly be said to convince readers that God's love is unconditional and everlasting and that Christ's atonement is universal and effectual? The Apostle John drew a beautiful word picture for us of the final outcome of God's love and Christ's atonement in which every created being in the whole universe is worshiping God and the sacrificial Lamb forever and ever (Rev. 5:13). **What a God— what a Savior—to whom be the glory in the church, in the world, and in the whole universe throughout eternity!**

The church's first systematic theologian, Origen (185-254), with no doubt, believed in the universal effectual atonement. Origen, his writings, and his memory were condemned in 553, long after Christianity had become the state religion of the Roman Empire.

This dastardly deed was done by the Fifth General Council, at the behest of the Roman Emperor, Justinian. **This, obviously, was three centuries after Origen's death!** This enabled control-freak emperors and power-hungry church officials to control the subjects of the Roman Empire through fear of eternal torture in literal hell fire. Eternal punishment in hell was made the official doctrine of the corrupt state church. Walker said of Origen, "No man of purer spirit or nobler aims ornaments the history of the ancient church."[1]

Sir Walter Scott (1771-1832) penned this truth: "Oh! What a tangled web we weave when first we practice to deceive!" This very tangled deceptive "theological web" is seen in the only two theologies accepted by so-called Orthodox Christianity since 553, though they flatly contradict each other on God's sovereignty and human free will but are unified in defending the insanity of eternal torture in hell. Today they are called Arminianism and Calvinism.

The Arminian Universal Provisional Atonement

The generally accepted view of Christ's atonement is that it was universal but provisional. "Universal" means that Christ died for everyone in general, but "provisional" means that he did not die for anyone in particular. What the universal but provisional view means is that, theoretically, every one could be saved or no one could be saved. That is because salvation depends on three things: 1. Hearing about God's plan of salvation in Christ during one's lifetime. 2. Personally accepting Christ as one's Savior before it is too late—before death. Catholics and Orthodox would say to be baptized rather than to "accept Christ." 3. In addition to accepting Christ and being baptized, Christians must also live a good enough life to be accepted into heaven when they die, because Christians can lose their salvation. Thus, entry into heaven is very "iffy!"

There are a lot of variations in beliefs within the universal provisional atonement. This is the view of Christ's atonement held by the vast majority of Christians whether Anglican, Catholic, Orthodox, or Protestant. Some Christian Churches do teach that salvation is by grace alone and that Christians cannot lose their salvation, but they are a small minority of all Christians.

In this view of the atonement, God's love is very conditional and time limited although proponents teach that God's love is unconditional and everlasting! It is conditional in that Christians

90

must live life well enough to be accepted into heaven, and they must evangelize the world. If they fail in their evangelism mission or they preach a perverted gospel, many people who might have been saved will end up in eternal hell fire.

According to some clergy, God will then stop loving those in hell so He can torture them forever, since God could not torture people if He loved them. This belief was preached by A.W. Tozer (1897-1963) who was an Evangelical pastor in The C & MA. Tozer stated that he had thought a lot about God's love and came to the conclusion that Satan sinned in such a way that God stopped loving him, and the day will come when God will stop loving those people whom He condemns to eternal hell fire.[2]

Some Christian writers have come to the logical conclusion that God, as a consuming fire (Deut. 4:24; Heb. 12:29) is the same as the fire of hell. The consuming fire of God consumes sin which purifies sinners. An example of this sane and sensible understanding is Dr. Sharon L. Baker. She wrote a very good book, *Razing Hell: Rethinking Everything You Have Been Taught about God's Wrath and Judgment*. But alas she came to an illogical conclusion. Baker said when all sin has been consumed there will be nothing good in some, so the fire will then annihilate them![3]

I stated in *SALTED WITH FIRE: Five Liberating Truths—The Gospel in a Nutshell* [chapter 8] that there will always remain the image of God. So all sinners will be purified, reconciled, and restored to God through His "fiery love!" In Julie Ferwerda's *Raising Hell: Christianity's Most Controversial Doctrine Put Under Fire*, the fire does purify sinners and annihilates no one.[4]

There is no place in *the Bible* where it says that God has ever stopped or ever will stop loving anyone. There is a problematic verse in which it says that God hated Esau (Rom. 9:13). This expression of disdain should be understood that God hated what Esau did in trading his birthright to his brother Jacob for a bowl of soup (Gen. 25). God did not treat Esau badly. In fact, God blessed Esau abundantly in material goods as Esau, himself, testified at his reunion with Jacob many years later (Gen. 33). But Esau could not have back his birthright, as the first-born son, though he later regretted having bartered it. We can say with certainty that Esau, who was a descendant of Abraham, will be saved, because "all Israel" shall be saved (Isa. 45:23-25; Rom. 11:26).

There is also the problematic teaching of Jesus who said that unless people hate their father and mother they cannot be His disciples. Some Biblical expositors have said that this means to love parents less than they love God. Dr. Rocco Errico, in his excellent book, *Let There Be Light*, gave a much better explanation based on the Aramaic meaning of the word translated "hate."[5]

John Gerstner (1914-1996) went even further than Tozer stating that God not only hates sin, as almost all Christians believe, but God also hates sinners.[6] This is why God will burn people in hell fire forever. It is absurd to believe that God's love will cease—God even hating sinners—so that He can torture people in hell forever.

It is equally absurd to believe that God will torture people in hell forever *even though He still loves them*, as most Christians who believe in eternal punishment contend. **But one of these three absurd views is true if hell is eternal! The doctrine of eternal torture in the fire of hell is logically indefensible. God's unconditional love and eternal torment is an oxymoron (# 3).**

Dr. John Gerstner believed in the view of John Calvin (1509-1564), and, of course, wrote from that perspective. Tozer wrote from the viewpoint of "Arminianism," named for Jacobus Arminius (1560-1609) another Protestant reformer who wrote in opposition to Calvinism. But these theological views predated Arminius and Calvin by centuries. John Wesley was influenced by Arminianism, and through Wesley's "Methodist Movement," much of Protestantism has so been influenced. Though they may or may not give it a name, these theological schools of thought, on the atonement of Christ, are present in Anglicanism, Catholicism, and Protestantism as well as some Eastern Orthodoxy in America.

The Calvinistic Limited Effectual Atonement

A minority view of Christ's atonement is that it was limited but effectual. "Limited" means that Christ did not die for every one; He died only for the "elect." *The Bible* does mention the "elect," but it does not say much about it, and nowhere does *the Bible* give the size of the "elect." Those who believe in the "elect" generally, with some exceptions, consider it to be a relatively small part of the human race and definitely does not include the fallen angels.

The limited nature of Christ's atonement, in this view, is a difficult theological pill to swallow, and most Christians do not swallow it, since it is very bitter in that no "unelect" person can be saved regardless of how good a life that person may have lived. For those who do swallow this Calvinistic pill, the really "sweet" part of the limited atonement is that Christ died for each and every member of the "elect" in particular. This view of the atonement is also called "The Particular" as well as "The Limited Atonement."

Since Christ died for each person of the "elect" in particular, it means that each and every one for whom Christ died will be saved. This is what the word "effectual" means—that Christ's atonement is 100 percent effective in getting every member of the "elect" saved. It is impossible for an elect person not to be saved, and it is impossible for an elect person to lose one's salvation. **Thus, the salvation of the elect is guaranteed!**

Those who believe in the limited effectual atonement cannot imagine that even one elect person will be forever lost or an unelect person be saved. Calvinists justify belief in the limited atonement by saying that God is sovereign. Saving only the "elect" would be unjust, but God cannot be unjust. The Judge of all the earth [per His nature] must do what is right (Gen. 18:23-33).

Calvinists are often very vocal about defending the doctrine of eternal punishment, but, even if this doctrine is true, from the Calvinistic perspective, it is "much to do about nothing," since no "elect" person will be lost and no "unelect" person will ever be saved. The "elect" are thus predestined for heaven while the "unelect" are predestinated for hell. Calvinists will strongly deny that they believe in "double predestination," which is merely a word game. They claim that God only predestinates for heaven, not hell. The obvious truth is that if God predestinates some only for heaven, every one else, by default, is predestinated for hell.

But I want to give credit where credit is due; the "particular atonement" is not all bad. In fact, it is a beautiful theological system except for the limited nature of Christ's atonement. **In addition to the effective part of the limited atonement and the security of the believer, there is another aspect of this view which is very appealing—the Holy Trinity acts in perfect harmony:** God, the Father, elects those to be saved; God, the Son, died for those to be saved; and God, the Holy Spirit, seeks the salvation of all those whom God chose and for whom Christ died with irresistible grace, so that every "elect" person will be saved.

As I stated, the Universal Provisional Atonement is very "iffy" while the Limited Effectual is systematic and leaves no one's salvation to chance. There is no place in *the Bible* which gives the size of the elect. The relative size of the elect is entirely a matter of conceptualization based on negative or positive thinking. Below are continuums which I have developed to illustrate this truth:

Calvinistic Continuum of the Size of the Elect

Small; Large; Almost All; All—Ultra-Universalism

Size of the Elect as Percentage of the Human Race

1-9%   10-49%   50-89%   90-99%   100%

Size of the Elect as Conceptualized by the Theological Cup

Almost Empty; Half Empty; Half Full; Almost Full; Full

These continuums may be self explanatory, but in case they are not, here is a brief explanation. Conceptualizing the size of the elect is truly a case of not seeing it as it is but seeing it as we are. "Small-Elect Calvinists" see the elect in single digits. The size of the elect in the thinking of "Large-Elect" Calvinists is more than 10% but less than 50%. Those who believe that the elect is more than half have broken the 50 percent conceptual barrier and may go up to 90%. From 90 to 99% these Calvinists are "Almost Universalists." With an elect of 100% they are Ultra-Universalists.

In fact, Neal Punt is a Calvinist who believes in a very large elect, and he has called his theology "Biblical Universalism."[7] He was not condemned as a heretic by his denomination for believing in universalism because he is not actually a Universalist—just, as a positive-thinking, very-large-elect Calvinist, almost one.

The early church, of course, believed in universal salvation, but universalism in America came out of the Calvinistic Churches in New England. These were positive-thinking Calvinists who interpreted such verses as God being the Savior of all people (I Tim. 4:10) and God sending the Son to be the Savior of the world as the elect being every one (I John 4:14). Thus, the "particular atonement" can get 100 percent of all people saved and still be a limited atonement if it applies only to the human race. But is the human race all God has in mind for salvation with the atonement of Christ? It definitely is not.

Christian Universalism sees God's redemptive plan, not just for the world but for the whole universe. It pleased God, through Christ, to reconcile all to Himself and make peace, by the blood of the cross, for those on earth and those, according to the Greek text, in the heavens ["the whole universe" *Good News Bible*], not just heaven (Col. 1:18-20). CU accounts for God's perfect plan of justice for all which explains the metaphorical use of hell fire. Calvinistic Ultra-Universalists do not believe in hell except for life on earth being hell. They just trust God to do the right thing. CU explains how God does the right thing.

Calvin died in 1564. The Council of Dort (1618-1619), meeting in the Netherlands, formally codified his theological position as the five points of Calvinism. The acrostic, using the word "TULIP" [very appropriate for the Dutch] was developed to convey these theological tenets. **The Universal Effectual Atonement combines the best features of the Universal Provisional and the Limited Effectual Atonement.**

Analyzing these four formulations of the "TULIP," one may ask, "Today, why does it matter what Calvinists believe?" The answer is that Calvinism seems to have little or no redeeming merit in light of believing only the elect can be saved, but this theology is very close to the truth of CU. The cover story of *Time Magazine* for March 12, 2009, was, "10 Ideas Changing the World Right Now." Idea # 3 is "The New Calvinism" by David Van Biema. He has an excellent way with words including a touch of humor:

> If you really want to follow the development of conservative Christianity, track its musical hits. In the early 1900s you might have heard "The Old Rugged Cross," a celebration of the atonement. By the 1980s you could have shared the Jesus-is-my-buddy intimacy of "Shine, Jesus, Shine." And today, more and more top songs feature a God who is very big, while we are...well, hark the David Crowder Band: "I am full of earth/ You are heaven's worth/ I am stained with dirt/ Prone to depravity." Calvinism is back, and not just musically. John Calvin's 16th century reply to medieval Catholicism's buy-your-way-out-of-purgatory excesses is Evangelicalism's latest success story, complete with an utterly sovereign and micromanaging deity, sinful and puny humanity, and the combination's logical consequence, predestination: the belief that before time's dawn, God decided whom he would save (or not), unaffected by any subsequent human action or decision.

Biema listed several of the best-known new or neo-Calvinists in Evangelical Christianity. Perhaps the most popular is Rev. Rick Warren who is best known for his best-selling book, *The Purpose Driven Life*.[8] I pointed out in *Spiritual Terrorism* Warren's belief that God is very active micromanaging every detail of people's lives. He stated that God does not just allow bad things to happen, God causes everything to happen. I stated that if this is true, God causes every war, murder, rape, robbery, etc. which gives all murderers, rapists, and robbers the perfect excuse for their crimes. Comedian Flip Wilson popularized the saying, "The Devil made me do it." But if Warren and other Calvinists are right, the perfect excuse for sinful and illegal behavior is, "God made me do it." I saw Rev. Warren interviewed by Larry King on CNN several years ago. King specifically asked Warren about his stated position that God causes everything. Warren replied that there is the problem of human free will. No, Rev. Warren cannot have it both ways; if God causes everything, people do not have free will. Conversely, if people have free will, God does not cause everything that happens. **Even God cannot have it both ways**. Logically, as I have stated, God can be fair or God can torture sinners forever, but God cannot be fair and torture sinners forever!

Fueling and Fanning Old Controversies

Biema addressed the passion on the religious right. He referred to Ted Olsen, a managing editor of *Christianity Today,* who said, "Everyone knows where the energy and the passion are in the Evangelical world," the implication being that it is coming from those who identify themselves as Calvinists. This kind of rhetoric is fueling and fanning old theological controversies between Calvinists and Arminians. This quote implies that the only valid interpretation of *the Bible* is a Calvinistic one. In that regard, Biema again quoted Mohler, "The moment someone begins to define God's being or actions biblically, that person is drawn to conclusions that are traditionally classified as Calvinist."

Biema wisely stated, "Of course, that presumption of inevitability has drawn accusations of arrogance and divisiveness since Calvin's time. Indeed, some of today's enthusiasts imply that non-Calvinists may actually not be Christians. Skirmishes among the Southern Baptists (who have a competing non-Calvinist camp) and online 'flame wars' bode badly." For readers who want more information, there are various websites with a Calvinistic orientation. One mentioned by Biema is "Between Two Worlds" as one of "cyber-Christendom's hottest links."

The 500th Anniversary of John Calvin's birthday was July 9, 2009. The era in which the Protestant Reformers lived was an age of great-religious intolerance! In Germany, Martin Luther admonished the rich land-owning "nobles" to give the dirt-poor peasants, who worked their lands, more than just starvation wages. When that did not happen, the poor workers rioted demanding a livable wage and protesting infant baptism. Luther, thinking this was going too far, sided with the "nobility." The peasant insurrection was stamped out with horrendous bloodshed[9] [70,000 to 100,000 peasants killed]!

In Geneva, Switzerland, at Calvin's behest, the ruling religious council condemned Michael Servetus as a heretic, principally, for not believing in the Trinity. Servetus, a Spaniard, was a brilliant man who was a physician and theologian. Since he was not a Swiss citizen, the worst that should have happened to him, due to his dispute with Calvin, was banishment. The council condemned Servetus and sentenced him to be burned at the stake. Calvin wanted to spare him the pain of the fire and recommended he be beheaded. He was burned to death using green wood to be slow and painful! The rationale was that such heretics needed to be executed to keep them from misleading others and causing them to be condemned to eternal hell fire along with the heretics who deceived them.[10]

Beyond belief in the Triune God, on some of the most significant theological issues, Calvinists and Arminians have opposite positions: the sovereignty of God vs. human free will, whether humans are partially or totally depraved, whether election is conditional or unconditional, whether Christ's atonement is universal or limited, whether saving grace is resistible or irresistible, and whether Christians can or cannot lose their salvation. An issue on which they are very solidly united in adamantly defending is the doctrine of eternal torture. Indeed, both theologies are a direct result of the false doctrine of eternal damnation. *If the doctrine of eternal torture is true*, **there is no way to reconcile the inherently contradictory, insanely absurd doctrine of eternal torture with God's unconditional love, infinite mercy, and perfect justice** [see oxymorons in chapter 1]!

Hopefully, we are not entering or are already in a new age of religious intolerance. What students are learning or not learning in the seminaries of America may hold the key to the future.

A Young Mind Closed to Seeking Truth

As mentioned, a very popular Calvinist, according to Biema, is Dr. Albert Mohler, President of Southern Seminary, a school of the 16-million-member Southern Baptist Convention which is the largest Protestant denomination in the USA. Mohler has become one of the "go-to guys" for the media who want to know what Evangelicals think in regard to a particular subject. I have seen Mohler interviewed several times on TV on religious issues. At one of my book signings for *Spiritual Terrorism*, a young man acted very interested in my book. As he read endorsements of it and some handout literature, we struck up an intermittent conservation as I signed books for others. He told me that he was a student at Southern Seminary.

I told him that I am aware the President, Dr. Mohler, is a Calvinist, and he stated that is true. I explained to him that Calvinism is actually very close to Christian Universalism and asked him if he would not, at least, like to learn another theological perspective which I had addressed in my book. After reading my book, if he did not agree, he would be able to refute CU more effectively. I told him that I would have loved to have learned this theology when I was his age because it would have saved me a lot of pain and suffering, and, more importantly, I would have been able to help even more victims of spiritual abuse during my lifetime of Christian ministry. He really seemed torn as to whether he should seek the truth. After discussing it for about half an hour, he just walked away. Having grown up in a Calvinistic Church and attending a seminary teaching Calvinism, he, apparently, decided to just stick with what he had always been and is being taught.

A Young Mind Seeking Truth

By contrast, a young woman who attended another book signing told me that she had graduated from college in the Spring and had enrolled in a reformed (Presbyterian) seminary for the Fall of that year. I asked her what she believed about the extent of salvation through Jesus, the Savior of the world. Apparently, she had been reared on Calvinism, but said she would like to believe every one is going to be saved. What compassionate person wouldn't? She also said she has been taught that the Christian Church has always taught eternal damnation, not universal salvation. I gave her the same handout information I had given the male seminary student and asked her if she would like to read it in *Spiritual Terrorism* [chapter 23]. This is a quote from Bishop Timothy Ware on the Eastern Orthodox Church's conception of hell, to purify, that was the teaching of the early church. She said, "Yes."

As soon as she had finished reading, without hesitation, she bought my book. That has been more than three years ago, so she has probably graduated from seminary and is now in Christian ministry. It would be interesting to know if she came to believe in Christian Universalism. If so, it would be gratifying to know how many victims of spiritual insanity she has already helped and will be able to help, in her lifetime of ministry, find peace with God, tranquility of mind, healing for damaged emotions, and joy of living. It would likewise be great to know how many other seminary students she may have positively influenced and how many people they may help be healed of spiritual insanity.

There could be no greater contribution to a tolerant and peaceful world than for Arminians and Calvinists to understand the fantastic truth of Christian Universalism, make peace with each other, and then work together to tear down walls and build bridges to adherents of other religions to live in peace and bring peace to our world torn by religious strife. My three theological acrostics, based on the "TULIP," are my contribution toward that end.

This is the formulation of Five-Point Calvinism. Notice, especially, the "L" for limited atonement.

> Five-Point Calvinism
> T-otal Depravity
> U-nconditional election
> L-imited Effectual Atonement
> I-rrestistible Grace
> P-erseverance of the Saints

The fatal flaw in Five-Point Calvinism is the limited atonement. By just understanding that the atonement is not limited but limitless, and then comprehending the truth that the elect are God's helpers to bring about the salvation of all, the "TULIP" acrostic is a systematic expression of universal salvation. Christ did not die only for the sins of the elect, as Calvinists believe, but also for the sins of the whole world (I Tim. 2:3-6; 4:10 and I John 4:14).

The difference between Five-Point Calvinism and Ultra-Universalism is only two words! Changing the word "limited" to limitless/unlimited seals the deal for the salvation of ALL, since the Calvinistic atonement is already effectual. Please note the "L" for limitless atonement—Ultra-Universalism—"no-hell" theology. But all believers will still experience the testing/refining fire at the Judgment Seat of Christ (I Cor. 3:10-15; II Cor. 5:10; Rom. 14:10).

Calvinism to Ultra-Universalism
T-otal Depravity
U-nconditional Election
L-imit[**less**] Effectual Atonement
I-rresistible Grace
P-erseverance of the Saints

The Ultra-Universalistic conception of salvation limits sinners reaping what they have sown, in regard to hurting other people, to this life only (Gal. 6:7). There is no "Great White Throne Judgment," and all enter into heaven. The Christian Universalistic "TULIP" does account for The Final Judgment and reaping exactly as what one has sown by adding the "S" to the acrostic making it plural, with the "S" representing, "salt of fire and burning sulfur."

Calvinism to Christian Universalism
T-otal Depravity [Trumped by God's Total Love]
U-nconditional Election [of Helpers to Save All]
L-imit[**less**] Effectual [Actually Saves All] Atonement
I-rresistible Grace [for All]
P-erseverance of the Saints [No One Can Lose Salvation]
S-alt of Fire and Burning Sulfur [Purification by Fire]

Salt of fire and burning sulfur are explained in chapter 5 on "Symbolism of Fire." If it is not clear you may want to, not just read but, study that chapter. As soon as people understand Jesus' mixed metaphor, "salted with fire" and the symbolism of "fire and brimstone/burning sulfur," they realize with crystal clarity that God's love is total—even trumping human depravity whether it is partial or total—and that Christ's atonement is both universal and effectual. This also means that God's saving grace is ultimately irresistible; all saints persevere, since no one can lose salvation.

Readers who want to read and learn more on systemic theology of universal salvation may want to read *Spiritual Terrorism* and study the verses in the acrostic, "Christian Universalism." The acrostic below depicts what non-systematic Arminianism looks like systematized in the form of "TULIPS," which leaves no one's salvation to chance as does traditional Arminianism.

Arminianism to Christian Universalism
T-otal Love of God [Trumps Depravity]
U-niversal Effectual [Actually Saves All] Atonement
L-amb of God Who Takes Away the Sin of the World
I-rresistible Grace [for All Created Beings]
P-erseverance of the Saints [No One Can Lose Salvation]
S-alt of Fire and Burning Sulfur [Purification by Fire]

There are some great hymns in the Christian faith which express God's total love in the grace of Christ who died for the sin of the whole world, not just an elect few. Eventually, all will confess their sins and profess faith in Christ the Savior of the whole world. An especially powerful song is, "Wonderful Grace of Jesus," by Haldor Lillenas (1885-1959). Just the first line of each of the three stanzas, plus the chorus are incomparable!

"Wonderful grace of Jesus, <u>Greater than all my sin</u>... **Reaching to all the lost...Reaching the most defiled**...Wonderful the matchless grace of Jesus, Deeper than the mighty rolling sea; Higher than the mountain, sparkling like a fountain, All-sufficient grace for even me, Broader than the scope of my transgressions,

Greater far than all my sin and shame; O magnify the precious name of Jesus, Praise His name!"

Christian hymns proclaim the total love of God in words and music in many ways. It would be great if Christians truly believed what they sing with such gusto. They sing of God's great love finding a way to redeem their souls and making them whole. God's love will be with all wayward children until all are loved back to wholeness through His amazing grace—divine love in action!

Views of Heaven

There is an old saying, "Everyone wants to go to heaven, but no one wants to go today." If Christians had a Biblical view of heaven, they might be interested in bringing heaven to earth. One's conception of God and heaven will determine one's love for God.

Heaven Can't Wait: Why rethinking the hereafter could make the world a better place, is an article by Jon Meacham, in *Time Magazine*, March 12, 2012. Meacham reported, according to a Gallup poll, 85% of Americans believe that life does not end with physical death. But there is a movement in Christianity, in America and Europe, to rethink concepts of heaven. A leading New Testament scholar in the endeavor is N.T. Wright, former Anglican bishop of Durham, England. Such scholars have asked two profound questions. "What if Christianity is not about enduring this sinful, fallen world in search of a reward of eternal rest? What if the authors of the New Testament were actually talking about a bodily resurrection in which God brings together the heavens and the earth in a wholly new, wholly redeemed creation?"

I grew up, as the vast majority of Christians have, on the view of earth and heaven expressed in the words of the old Christian hymn, "I'll Fly Away." "Some glad morning when this life is o'er, I'll fly away to my home on God's celestial shore. I'll fly away." Or, "This world is not my home; I'm just passing through. My treasure is laid up somewhere beyond the blue." The orientation is "other worldly"—escapism, to leave this sin-filled world, to go to a "better place." How many times have you heard Christians say in regard to the death of a loved one, "He or she is in a 'better place'"?

Again, Meacham quoted Wright who is now *the New Testament* expert at the University of St. Andrews. "When 1st century Jews spoke about eternal life, they weren't thinking of going to heaven in the way we normally imagine it...Eternal life meant the age to come, the time when God would bring heaven and earth together, the time when God's kingdom would come and his will would be done on earth as in heaven."

This view is in total agreement with the petition in The Lord's Prayer which Christians around the world pray every Sunday. "Thy kingdom come, Thy will be done on earth as it is in heaven." Remember, this is the prayer which our Lord taught us to pray. Did He teach us to pray thusly for nothing—needlessly? Of course, conservative Christians relegate peace on earth to the millennial reign of Christ after His Second Advent. But earth and heaven being one may not have to wait for that event. Meacham explained:

> After Jesus failed to inaugurate the new kingdom in the lifetimes of the disciples and early apostles, subsequent generations of Christians—now two millennia's worth— were left to speculate about the nature of life after death. And the further believers have moved in time from the New Testament era, the further many Christians have moved from New Testament understandings about heaven. The power of poets and artists, of Dante and Michelangelo, created indelible images; the fiery story of Revelation, though problematic and highly metaphorical, has long been taken too literally.

The view of God transforming the world into heaven on earth, has far-reaching implications. It is right up there with saving the environment being as important as saving souls. There is another old saying, "Some Christians are so heavenly minded, they are no earthly good." Protecting the environment, nuclear disarmament, social justice, world peace, etc. may resonate with young people turned off with the church's present emphasis on soul saving.

Almost all conservative Christians have bought lock, stock, and barrel into the Futuristic View, end-of-the-world fatalism, of the Revelation. There are other historical interpretations of the Revelation, but the one which makes the most sense to me is the Idealistic View. This interpretation holds that the Revelation is not predictive prophecy but a very vivid dramatization of the aeon/age-long conflict between good and evil, which is applicable to every generation but is specific to none. God, not man, is sovereign. William Newell (1868-1956) captured the essence of CU in his great hymn, "At Calvary." In the fourth stanza he wrote, "Oh, the love that drew salvation's plan! Oh, the grace that brought it down to man! Oh, the mighty gulf that God did span at Calvary!" Thus, God will ultimately destroy evil (I John 3:8) and reconcile the world to Himself (II Cor. 5:17-21). This is the ultimate outcome of God's grace—divine love—total love in action!

God has vested every created being with incredible dignity! Since God will never violate anyone's free will, He has given each and every one a **veto** over His grand and glorious goal of becoming "all in all" [KJV]—"everything to every one" [RSV] (I Cor. 15:28)! Please note that the RSV used the words "every one," meaning each and every person, not just "everyone" in general. As long as even one person continues to say "No" to God's never-withdrawn offer of salvation, God will not be all in all. Only when the last holdout has freely said, "Yes," to living in submission to God and in harmony with all created beings will God be all in all! Imagine the universe without even a trace of evil, when sin has been consumed, and every sinner has been reconciled to God.

Then and only then will God be everything to every one! This is what it means for God to be: not all in a few, all in many, or even all in almost all but ALL IN ALL! This will herald the glorious dawn of universal submission and confession (Isaiah 45:23-25; 66:23; Rom. 14:9-11; Phil. 2:9-11), universal peace (Isaiah 2:4; 11:6-9), and universal worship (Rev. 5:13)!

Discussion Questions

1. What do you believe about the nature of God? In terms of love, grace, mercy, and perfect justice?

2. Do you believe in the Arminian view of the atonement which is universal but provisional? Why or why not? What does "provisional" atonement mean? Is Arminianism confusing? Explain.

3. Do you believe in the Calvinistic view of the atonement which is limited to only the elect? Does that make sense to you? Why or why not?

4. Do you understand the Five-Point Calvinistic Acrostic? Explain.

5. Do you believe in the Christian Universalist view of Christ's atonement? Does it make sense to you? Why or why not? Explain.

6. What does it mean for Christ to die effectually?

7. How does your conception of God influence or dictate your view of Christ's atonement? Explain.

8. Which view of the atonement is most reflective of God's unconditional love, amazing grace, infinite mercy, and perfect justice? Explain your rationale.

9. Had you heard of the concept of God giving every person a veto over His goal of becoming all in all (I Cor. 15:28)? Does this vest each and every one with incredible dignity? Why or why not?

Chapter 7
Inspiration to be Like God

The second "I" in the acrostic "CHRISTIANITY" represents "Inspiration to be Like God," the greatest impetus to love, worship, and serve God. What is the strongest motivator of human behavior fear, hate, or love? Most Christian pastors, by their preaching, believe that it is fear of God due to eternal damnation in hell fire. A hell-fire-preaching pastor on TV preached, through clenched teeth, "You must fear God, fear God, fear God for when you fear God [enough] you will love God!"

Being Spiritually Perfect

In this regard, Matthew 5:48 has been used to terrorize many Christians who have been spiritually abused by the insanity in Christianity of literalism and legalism. Legalism is salvation by keeping The Ten Commandments and all the religious rules of the church. In this verse, Jesus said, **"Be ye therefore perfect, even as your Father which in heaven is perfect" (KJV)**.

Rocco A. Errico has two doctorates, a Doctor of Philosophy Degree and a Doctor of Theology Degree. Dr. Errico has devoted most of his life to studying the Aramaic language which Jesus spoke. In his very illuminating book, *And There Was Light,* he gave this enlightening insight in regard to the word "perfect" as understood in the Aramaic. "Most of us usually equate being 'perfect' with total flawlessness and infallibility, but the Aramaic term does not imply any such notion. Many of us labor under the idea that we must be perfect. The Aramaic word 'gmeera' does mean 'perfect,' but in the sense of 'complete,' 'through,' 'finished,' 'full-grown,' 'mature,' 'accomplished,' 'comprehensive,' 'rounded out,' and 'all–inclusive,' In the Near East when a young man arrives at full maturity, he is a 'gmeera' —'a man of understanding.' It also refers to anyone who is very thorough in whatever she or he does."[1]

Per Errico, Jesus' disciples were to be inclusive, not exclusive, in their love and approach to others. The idea of "outsiders" versus "insiders" was not to be a part of their vocabulary. Before Jesus told his disciples to become perfect, he had taught them:

> Love your enemies, bless anyone who curses you, do good to anyone who hates you, and pray for those who carry you away by force and persecute you, so that you may be sons of your Father who is in heaven, who causes the sun to shine upon the good and the bad, and who pours down his rain upon the just and the unjust.

Dr. Errico explained, "This is the perfection to which Jesus referred. And just as God does not discriminate but is 'all-inclusive,' so his children were to show the same nonexclusive nature as their 'heavenly Father.' Jesus makes no demands upon humans to be flawless or infallible. Perfection is a loving presence. It is the loving presence that is all-inclusive. This loving presence knows no sex, race, color, creed, barriers, or boundaries. Each stage of human development is its own perfection. A loving presence is a presence where harmony, peace, and joy manifest in one's heart and mind. This is God in action. Jesus encouraged his disciples to accept and treat everyone in the same manner as God blesses the good and the bad, the just and the unjust."[2]

God's "Crazy" Love

Francis Chan wrote a very good book titled, *Crazy Love*,[3] in which he shared that he was abused and neglected by his father as he was growing to adulthood. He related that he spent a lot of time trying to hide from his father in order not to be abused by him. Chan stated that he did not understand the love of God until after his first child, a daughter, was born. Only then, according to Chan, was he able to understand the love of God for himself as well as the love of God for all people.

The problem with Chan, it seems, is that he doesn't truly believe the wonderful things he wrote concerning the "crazy" love of God,

109

especially the title of his book, *Crazy Love*. The evidence that Chan does not believe what he has written is that he believes in the doctrine of eternal damnation in hell fire for all people who have not accepted Jesus Christ, in this life, as their Lord and Savior. In fact, Chan has written another book by the title *Erasing Hell*,[4] in which he labors in explaining and justifying the horrible doctrine of eternal damnation in hell but concludes that *the Bible* actually teaches it. If Chan truly believes what he wrote about the wonderful, all-encompassing, all-inclusive love of God, he would logically have to conclude that the doctrine of eternal punishment in hell cannot be true. Torturing one's disobedient children in fire is not something a loving parent would do. Readers, would you?

Examples of Mature Human Love and Forgiveness

A great example of mature love and forgiveness is Nelson Mandela. Mandela, a black man, grew up in the country of South Africa with a small white minority ruling and oppressing the large population of black people. This government practiced apartheid— complete racial segregation. The ruling powers governed with an iron fist and tolerated no dissent. Mandela joined and became president of The African National Congress whose purpose was to end apartheid and set up a democratic government in which all people would be treated equally. He was arrested and charged with conspiracy against the government for his antiapartheid activities. He was convicted and imprisoned where he spent 27 years. Mandela was finally released from prison, apartheid was ended, and he became the president of democratic South Africa.

Typically, when an oppressive government is overthrown and a new government comes to power, there is a blood bath of the oppressors by those who were being oppressed. In fact, many whites fled the country fearing there would be massive retribution. That did not happen in South Africa largely due to Mandela's leadership. He just wanted the small white minority to acknowledge the wrongs they had done and apologize to the large black majority. Bishop Desmond Tutu led truth and reconciliation commissions to confront the oppressors and facilitate national healing. This is one of the best examples of love and forgiveness in the history of the world! Another great example of forgiveness is elderly American and Japanese as well as German veterans of World War II, who were mortal enemies, shaking hands and embracing each other. If human beings can be this loving, magnanimous, and forgiving of their enemies, what more will God, in love, do? God, according to *the Bible*, is not just loving, God is love (1 John 4:8). Thus, God will love, forgive, and reconcile all sinners who have violated His moral law and hurt others in the human family!

The Great and Greatest Emancipator

President Abraham Lincoln (1809-1865) is known as "The Great Emancipator" due to freeing the slaves during the Civil War. He was inspired by Jesus who freed all people from their sins. **Lincoln's key verse of Holy Scripture was I Cor. 15:22, "For as in Adam all die, even so in Christ shall all be made alive."** He logically and correctly concluded that whatever harm Adam had caused the human race, was all corrected in Christ, the Redeemer and Savior of the world. In his Second Inaugural Address on March 4, 1865, he compassionately declared, "With malice toward none, with charity for all ...let us...bind up the nation's wounds, to do all which may achieve and cherish a just and lasting peace...." If The Great Emancipator, with human failings, was so compassionate as to declare, a few weeks before the end of the Civil War, "Malice toward none and [love] for all," how much more will Christ, The Greatest Emancipator, at the end of the war between good and evil, proclaim hatred for none and love for all!

During the Civil War word leaked that President Lincoln was going to appoint Rev. James Shrigley (1813-1905), a Universalist minister to be an army chaplain. Hearing this, some Protestant clergymen traveled to Washington, D.C., to protest to Lincoln. When asked why they were opposed to his appointment, they replied that he believed that everyone will be saved including the southern rebels. Lincoln replied that he could think of no better recommendation than that, so he made the appointment!

111

Judgment by our loving Lord will be only for correction so it will be proportional, totally fair, and perfectly just. At the end of the war between good and evil all spiritual rebels will be back home in the family of God living peacefully with all created beings and worshiping God and the Lamb eternally (Rev. 5:13)!

A Great Humanitarian

Francis of Assisi, Italy, was born in 1182 and died in 1226 at the age of only 44, but he accomplished much during his short lifetime. Per online research, he was born into a wealthy family and spent his young adult years partying and was called "The King of Feasts." Later he forsook that lavish lifestyle because he heard the call of God to devote his life to helping the masses of unfortunate people. The world into which he was born had a lot in common with the world today: violence, war, greed, oppression of the poor, etc. Desiring to truly be an instrument of God's love and peace, his work led to the founding of the Catholic Order that still bears his name—"The Franciscans." St. Francis' ideals live on in this order and in Christians, as a whole, who seek to inspire the truth of The Gospel of peace and justice throughout the world.

Mother Teresa attributed significance to this prayer of St. Francis in accepting the Nobel Peace Prize in 1979. In 1984 Archbishop Desmond Tutu, from South Africa, in accepting his award of the Nobel Peace Prize, shared that it is an important part of his devotions. President Bill Clinton quoted from this prayer in welcoming Pope John Paul II to New York for the Pope's address at the United Nations in 1995. This is St. Francis' prayer which has been adapted in various spoken and musical forms.

Prayer of Saint Francis of Assisi

Lord, make me an instrument of your peace.
Where there is hatred, let me sow love;
where there is injury, pardon;
where there is doubt, faith;

where there is despair, hope;
where there is darkness, light;
and where there is sadness, joy.

O Divine Master, grant that I may not so much seek
to be consoled as to console;
to be understood as to understand;
to be loved as to love.
For it is in giving that we receive;
it is in pardoning that we are pardoned;
and it is in dying that we are born to eternal life. Amen.

What Would Loving Human Parents Do?

I have stated many times that virtually every theological problem can be resolved by thinking in terms of the loving father/child or mother/child relationship. From the time my children were born, I loved my son and my daughter so much that I would have done anything, even including laying down my life for them, in order to protect them. There is no way I could have intentionally abused or neglected them.

When my son was about five years of age, I had taken my family to a church conference that lasted for a week. My wife would attend the evening services with our children but not attend the meetings during the day, especially business meetings. Sometimes she would take our children to a park, movie, or shop.

One afternoon, when I was going to a business meeting, my son wanted to go with me rather than go with his mother and sister. I said to him, "Honey, I would love to have you go with me, but the meeting is going to be very long and, for you, probably very boring." He said, "I know, Daddy, but I want to be with you." I replied, "The business meeting I am sure is going to be very long and boring. Are you sure you want to attend?" He looked up at me and said so preciously, "Yes, Daddy, I just want to be with you!"

113

Wow, to warm a father's heart that is fantastic! He did go with me, was well behaved, and slept through half of the meeting sitting on my lap with his head on my shoulder. What a blessed experience! As he grew into adolescence and then his teen years, it was even more precious when he went from saying, "Daddy, I want to be with you" and also started saying, "Daddy, I want to be like you!" For a loving devoted father, that is as good as it gets!

When my daughter was only three years old, I had to discipline her for picking on her brother. When she got out of timeout, she came to me, climbed up on my lap, and said, with fire in her eyes, "Daddy, I hate you!" She was so cute and deadly serious that I could hardly keep from laughing. I wanted to validate rather than be dismissive of her feelings. So I said to her, "Honey, you don't actually hate daddy, you hate what I did." She replied, with the seriousness of a heart attack, "No, I hate you too!" Again, I could hardly keep from laughing, but I decided to try again. I said, "Honey, I realize that right now you feel like you hate not only what daddy did, but you feel like you hate me too. But tomorrow will be different, tomorrow you will love daddy." She looked at me again straight in the eye and said with the same deadly seriousness, "No, tomorrow I'll hate you too!"

Then, perhaps feeling a sense of estrangement, she said something very significant, "Hold me, Daddy." I kissed her on her forehead and cuddled her in my arms until she fell asleep. I then carried her to her bedroom, tucked her into bed, kissed her on the cheek, and whispered in her ear, "Honey, I love you."

The next morning my daughter came to me, climbed up on my lap, hugged me around the neck, kissed me on my cheek, and said tenderly, "Daddy, I love you!" If I, as less than a perfect earthly father, could understand the emotions my daughter was experiencing, and allow her to express true feelings, without retribution or rejection, how much more will our heavenly Father, who is perfect, understand the feelings of His children? Jesus, who spoke Aramaic, called God "Abba," which means daddy (Mark 14:36).

Is God a Christian?

Many children are taken to Sunday school and church by their loving parents who want them to learn faith and values so they will grow up to be good persons, love God, help others, and go to heaven when this life is over. Sadly, many of these children hear messages concerning God about which are very frightening and are totally unlike any loving parent and any compassionate human being.

Allan Chevrier wrote an enlightening book I have already recommended, *Whatever Became of Melanie?*[5] on Christian Universalism which is the logical outcome of God's unconditional and everlasting love. This author related the story of a Sunday school teacher who taught the class members that, as Christians, we are commanded by God to love our neighbors as ourselves, forgive those who hurt us, do good for people who do us wrong, and even love our enemies! The children were then told by this Sunday school teacher that all people must confess their sins and accept Jesus into their hearts before they die or God will judge them, condemn them, and throw them into the literall fire in hell wherein they will be tormented day and night forever and ever! **A young girl spoke up and innocently expressed the absurdity of what she had just been taught about God. She exclaimed, "I think God should become a Christian."** No, God is not a Christian which is merely an adjective to describe one who is a follower of Christ, the Messiah. But God is certainly no hypocrite!

God Practicing What God Preaches

Matthew 5:48 is one of the most misunderstood verses in the whole Bible. As I referenced it in the first chapter, "Christianity With Insanity," this verse has often been, and still is used, to terrorize men, woman, and children. Per the KJV, "Be ye, therefore, perfect even as your Father in heaven is perfect." Taken out of context and coupled with the false doctrine of eternal torture in hell fire, this verse has struck fear into the hearts of Christians, especially children. What is the context?

In the preceding verses (38-47), Jesus taught His followers not to retaliate when wronged, turn the other check, go the second mile, lend to those in need even if they couldn't pay it back, love one's neighbor as oneself, love one's enemies, bless those who cursed them, do good for those who hated them, and pray for those who persecuted and despitefully used them. Why live and love like this? So they could be children like our heavenly Father who causes the sun to shine on the evil and the good and causes the rain to fall on the just and the unjust. God even demonstrated His love for us by coming in Christ and dying for us while we were yet unrepentant sinners—His spiritual enemies (Rom. 5:6-8).

When, in context, people understand this all-inclusive love of God, they will be motivated to love, live, and forgive like Jesus did and taught us to do. Thus, when people learn that hell is not literal fire but is metaphorical fire symbolizing purification of every one, people will respond in the same matchless love for God and all humanity.

Context of the Word "Perfect" and Perfect Love

The Apostle John wrote, "There is no fear in love; but perfect love casts out fear: because fear has torment. The one who fears has not been made perfect in love" (1 John 4:18). Commenting on this verse, Dr. Rocco Errico, in his enlightening book, *And There Was Light*, on the Aramaic Language Jesus spoke, explained: "We all have our own ideas of what it means when we use the word 'perfect.' This is especially true when we talk about 'perfect love' or a 'perfect relationship.' For most people, this word 'perfect' can be a troublesome term. It seems that many of us suffer under the tyranny of trying to become perfect. We labor under the idea of trying to live a perfect life."[6]

Per Errico, "John, in his letter, uses the Aramaic term mshamlya, coming from the root word mla. Its verbal origin means 'to fill, replenish, complete, conclude,' and also 'to come to full growth.' Thus, John describes love as 'complete,' 'mature,' or 'whole.' He qualifies this love as a love that is mature, rounded

116

out—a love that is all-inclusive." Errico goes on to explain, "Love, in its nature, is always loving. Hooba, 'love,' comes from the Aramaic root habor hav. It means 'to set on fire' and 'to burn fiercely,' that is, 'to burn so strongly that it turns white hot.' Scripture tells us that 'God is love.' (See 1 John 4:8.) Throughout Holy Scripture, various biblical authors symbolize the presence of God as 'fire.' Some writers refer to God as a 'consuming fire'...Fire is also a symbol for transformation."[7]

This is Errico's beautiful summation, "God's presence is nothing but pure love (hooba). The Spirit of God is the most compassionate, 'white hot,' fiery presence we can experience. This love does not discriminate, for it loves everyone the same. (See Matthew 5:44-47)...Love is so intense, powerful, and 'white hot' that we cannot really describe it at all. Most of the deep things in life often lack definition. This is because they go beyond words and mental comprehension, but never beyond our apprehension. We can apprehend love because love apprehends us! It is the source of our nature—a living energy. Try though we may, we cannot run from it...But a complete, mature love does not fear anything because it is an all-inclusive love. And an all-inclusive love is God."[8]

All-Inclusive Love Include Those Who Die A Suicide?

Almost all Christians, it appears, have been taught that suicide is "self murder," so it is not only a sin but is a sin for which a person will be condemned forever to the fire of hell. Here is another glaring example of spiritual insanity. Christians who teach this foolishness, which insults and negates the love and grace of God, also teach that murder is a forgivable sin, since the murderer is alive to confess this horrible sin and ask God for forgiveness which God will grant. In regard to suicide, the "reasoning" is that a person cannot be forgiven before the deed, and there is no time to confess after having done so. But forgiveness depends on the loving nature of God, not on whether a person had time to repent or said exactly the "right" words. On the cross, as a dying utterance, Jesus prayed for the forgiveness of His executioners, and they had not even asked for forgiveness (Luke 23:34)!

Jesus said that they didn't know what they were doing. Yes, they understood intellectually but not spiritually. Neither did the people, who were mentally ill or so emotionally distraught that they died a suicide, know what they were doing. Surely, God's unconditional love, which burns with white hotness, will love them to health and wholeness as an integral part of the human family!

I included a whole chapter on suicide in my book, *Spiritual Terrorism*. Since writing my book, I have gotten involved in attending some meetings of "Messages of Hope" for family members who have lost loved ones to suicide. Every situation is a gut-wrenching, nerve-shattering, heart-rending experience! The participants have told me that I have helped them, but they have also helped me to have greater understanding. For example, they have shared that it is emotionally painful for terms to be used such as "committed suicide" and "taken one's life." This seems to imply some rational act when suicide is not something which is rationally done. It is better to say "Died a suicide." When doing the second edition of *Spiritual Terrorism* I will thus reword such terms.

The title of that chapter in *Spiritual Terrorism* is, "Better Than God?" which included the wonderfully healing poem by Peggy Kociscin, "Better Than God???"[9] I share it here because it has been such a fantastic blessing to families who have lost a loved one to suicide and to other families who were not sure of the eternal destiny of their deceased loved ones. This is true of hospice families, those in my private counseling practice, those in a psychiatric hospital, and Master-Degree students in a course I developed and taught at Marshall University Graduate College on spiritual abuse.

This poem is about Peggy's son who died a suicide. She has given me permission and her blessing to use it. May this lovely lady continue to be blessed knowing that her spiritually insightful poem continues to bless many people.

Better Than God???
By Peggy Kociscin

The day you died, my mind, my heart became obsessed by fear.
Where are you? Did a hell now claim the son I hold so dear?
For I recalled the "thou shalt nots" instilled within my brain;
Will judgment for the failure mean an everlasting pain?

Addiction gained control of you (a rebel through and through);
Appalled and hurt, my heart would break at things you'd say and do.
But through my fear, God came to me and touched me tenderly.
He smiled, and with a loving voice He kindly spoke to me.

Did you love your son no matter what? "Certainly," I said.
"Did you forgive him for the pain for all the things he did?"
"Of course," I said, "He is my son, how could I not forgive him?
An unconditional mother's love was all I had to give him."

I thought I heard God chuckle then as He whispered His reply,
"Why would you think that you can love more perfectly than I?"
Chastised, ashamed, I understood, all doubt and fear now ceased;
My son is in the hands of God in glory and at peace.
I find that I can let him go and the pain is now abating;
For I know that when I meet my God my John will be there...
    waiting.

This poet, without any theological education, has a far better conception of God and a much better grasp on grace than all those who are preaching and teaching eternal damnation whether they be doctors of theology, pastors, priests, bishops, or even the Pope. She, like God, understands a mother's unconditional love that the prophet Isaiah compares to the tenderness of a nursing mother (49:15). Perhaps because I had a wonderful mother whose love was truly unconditional, I especially love the message of Peggy's poem as well as Kipling's poem, "O Mother O Mine." This poem characterizes a mother's love as being so unfailing and powerful that, if possible, it would love back to wholeness a wayward child who was executed and damned in body and soul. If a mother's

119

love is that great, how much greater must God's love be, since God is the source of all love?

While the Roman Catholic Church teaches that suicide is a mortal [eternal] sin, it also teaches that God might grant "salutary [after-death] repentance" to those who have died a suicide. God not only can but will grant salutary—healing—repentance, even after death, for all still in need of His saving grace. **God's perfect love will be with all wayward children until all are loved back to wholeness through His amazing grace!**

Literalism Not Inspire Believers to be Like God

On August 14, 2011, I heard the Rev. Dr. John Hagee, a self-confessed literalist, preaching on national TV. He stated that *The Holy Bible* must be taken literally. He thus received applause from his mega-church congregation. He then went on preaching and declared, in regard to the beauty of Jesus, that He is the "Lily of the Valley," the "Rose of Sharon," the "Bright Morning Star," and the "Alpha and the Omega!" I thought, "Rev. Hagee, did you not hear or not believe what you just preached—that *the Bible* must be taken literally? Jesus is not literally a flower, a star in the sky, nor the first and last letters of the Greek alphabet."

Literalists say that every word in *the Bible* is literally true. They obviously do not understand symbolic language, of which there is much in *the Bible*, or else they would not be literalists. Anthropomorphically [ascribing human characteristics to God or inanimate things], will mountains sing and trees clap their hands (Isa. 55:12)? And will mountains skip like rams and hills skip like lambs (Psalm 114:4)? Hyperbolically [gross exaggeration for humor], has anyone ever swallowed a camel (Mt. 23:24)? Metaphorically [one thing representing another], is God, who is a consuming fire (Deut. 4:24; Heb. 12:29), on fire? Allegorically [an extended metaphor], was Jonah literally swallowed by a whale [actually a big fish] (1:17)? A literalist stated that he would believe *the Bible* even if it should have said that Jonah swallowed the whale! I marvel at such blind and mindless slavery to literalism!

The above examples are obvious literary devices which no person with at least an ounce of common sense takes literally. Sometimes the truth is not obvious, as literalists contend. This truth is illustrated with John 14:6 in which Jesus said, "I am the way, the truth, and the life: no man cometh unto the Father, but by me." Fundamental and Evangelical Christians often quote this verse in support of the false doctrine of eternal punishment in hell. In fact, they would say that this verse, like the rest of *the Bible*, needs no interpretation—just accept what it clearly says.

In the search for deeper spiritual truth, I called and discussed this with a long-time friend, Rabbi Victor Urecki, who is fluent in Hebrew in which *The Torah* [Christians know as *the Old Testament*], was written. I told Rabbi Urecki that I am aware *The Torah* was called by Jews, "The Way." I asked if *The Torah* [meaning "teaching"] was also known as "the truth" and "the life." He sent me an email with the copy of a prayer Jews always pray before reading *The Torah*, "Thank you O Lord for giving us *The Torah* of truth which sets before us the way of everlasting life." So there you have it—the WAY, the TRUTH, and the LIFE.

The deeper truth, not the superficial, is Jesus was saying that He was the embodiment of *The Torah*. Rabbi Urecki stated that a rabbi as the embodiment of *The Torah* would have been a common understanding among Jews. He explained that, in the ancient world, the rabbi would have been one of the few and, perhaps, the only person in a village or community who could read and write. When the rabbi had learned *The Torah* well, and in many cases had memorized all of it, he would have been understood to be the embodiment of *The Torah*.

Rabbi Jesus said, "Search the Scriptures...for they testify of me" (John 5:39). "The Scriptures" would be *The Torah* since, when Jesus spoke these words, *The New Testament* was not yet written. Jesus was saying that people come to God through the whole truth of the word of God in *The Torah*. He was not setting forth a new exclusive way to God that would result in the eternal damnation of the vast majority of the human race all of whom He died to save!

Remember, Jesus also declared that were He lifted up from the earth, on the cross, He would draw all persons to Himself (John 12:32). **This dynamic is what I have called, "The Spiritual Magnetism of Christ."** Metal has no power to attract itself to a magnet. A magnet just naturally draws metal to itself. Christ is in the process of drawing all to Himself and, ultimately, will be 100 percent effective in fulfilling His stated purpose.

The World Angry with or in Love with God?

As I explained in *Spiritual Terrorism,* at one time or other, almost everyone in the world is angry with God over the death of a loved one, loss of love, loss of job, loss of health, loss of financial security, loss of home, being the victim of a crime, etc. But some glorious day, every created being in the whole universe will, in turn, sit on God's lap and say, "Daddy, I love you!"

Today, many of God's children are out of fellowship with Him, pursuing their own selfish desires. They are modern prodigal sons and daughters who think they are having a good time doing their own thing and sometimes hurting others. They are, however, merely in the process of learning that sin promises pleasure but produces pain.

Eventually, each and every prodigal daughter and son will return to our heavenly Father's home and say, "Daddy, I just want to be with you, be like you, and live in peace with every one else in our whole family of God!" Bill Gaither wrote, "The Family of God," which could be the theme song for universal reconciliation. It proclaims: "I'm So Glad I'm Part of the Family of God...." Don't you wish every one were? How wonderful it will be when every one is living peacefully in "The Family of God!"

Discussion Questions

1. What did you understand about being "perfect," Per Matthew 5:48 before reading this book? How do you understand it now?

2. What does the word "perfect" mean in Aramaic the language spoken by Jesus?

3. In what sense can our love be perfect like God's?

4. What does Chan mean by God's "crazy" love? If it is "crazy" in this sense, how can it exclude anyone?

5. How is Nelson Mandela a great example of mature love and human forgiveness? Since a human can forgive this much, what about God?

6. Are you inspired by the prayer of St. Francis of Assisi? In what way? To do what in God's service?

7. How can thinking of God's love in terms of parental love solve virtually every theological problem?

8. Do you believe that God is a Christian? Why or why not? What does being a Christian mean to you?

9. How might you apply the concept of President Abraham Lincoln, as "The Great Emancipator," to freeing people in spiritual bondage today?

10. When Jesus has done what He came to do—free all people from fear of death (Heb. 2:15) and has done what He said that He will do—draw all people to Himself (John 12:32) will not He be "The Greatest Emancipator" of time and eternity? Does this view threaten or strengthen your Christian faith? Why?

Chapter 8
Ambassadors of Peace For Christ

The "A" in the acrostic "CHRISTIANITY" represents "Ambassadors of Peace for Christ." After Jesus' crucifixion, burial, and resurrection, He appeared to His disciples and gave them their mission. Saint Matthew recorded, "And Jesus came and spoke unto them, saying, 'All power is given unto me in heaven and in earth. Go, therefore, and teach all nations, baptizing them in the name of the Father, and of the Son, and of the Holy Spirit: Teaching them to observe all things whatsoever I have commanded you: and, lo, I am with you always, even unto the end of the aeon/age'" [world, KJV] (28:18-20). This mission given to the apostles by the Lord Jesus Christ has become known as "The Great Commission." Throughout the centuries, the Christian Church, mission organizations, and individual Christians have diligently tried to fulfill this command of our Lord.

The Apostle, Paul, admonished the Christians at the church in Corinth, Greece. "Therefore, if any man be in Christ, he is a new creature: old things are passed away; behold, all things are become new. And all things are of God, who has reconciled us to himself by Jesus Christ, and has given to us the ministry of reconciliation: To wit, that God was in Christ, reconciling the world unto himself, not imputing their trespasses unto them; and has committed unto us the word of reconciliation. Now then we are ambassadors for Christ, as though God did beseech you by us...be reconciled to God" (II Cor. 5:17-20).

Many Christian Churches and parachurch organizations have developed evangelistic literature, in the form of tracts, booklets, and pamphlets in order to help Christians to be able to share their faith—The Gospel. The word "gospel," in Greek, means good news. The message of Christian Universalism is truly Good News for all people, not just an "elect" few or just those people who have been fortunate enough to hear the Gospel message in this life. This news, for everyone in the whole world—past, present, and future—is so good that I capitalize the "G" and "N" in "Good News!"

Some evangelistic materials are much better than others, from a positive or negative perspective, but virtually all are very negative—"turn or burn!" In essence, the message is that Jesus, God in the flesh, died to make it possible for all people to be saved, but in order to be saved, people must hear about salvation in Christ, acknowledge that they are sinners, confess their sins, and personally accept Jesus as their Lord and Savior. If they do not hear and do so in this life, at The Final Judgment, God will judge them, condemn them, and cast them into hell fire wherein they will be tormented day and night forever!

The Anglican, Orthodox, Catholic, and mainline Protestant Churches would say that people must be baptized in order to be saved. These churches baptize infants who, as older children, are enrolled in confirmation classes at the end of which they personally confirm the Christian faith as their own. But what about those who grow up and never confirm the Christian faith? Are they then lost? What about those who did confirm the Christian faith and as adults renounced it or even became atheists?

The late well-known atheist, Christopher Hitchens, was a Christian before renouncing Christianity and his faith in God. [Here is irony: "Christopher," in Greek, means "Christ bearer."] He wrote the book, *god is not Great: How Religion Poisons Everything*.[1] By the way, the lower case "g" for God is not a typo. It is how Hitchens, who died in December of 2011, referred to God in whom he did not believe. I have his book which is very well researched and written. Having read it carefully, I am confident I understand why he became an atheist.

From my knowledge of history, I agree with at least ninety percent of what Hitchens said about religion poisoning everything. Rather than saying that religion poisons everything, I would say that fear-based religion is spiritually terroristic and spiritually insane. Spiritual terrorism, spiritual insanity, and religious poison are synonymous terms. The problem is not religion but the misunderstanding and misuse of religion.

A fatal flaw in Hitchens' understanding is that Jesus believed in eternal punishment. Other writers have made the same mistake. Bertrand Russell wrote the book, *Why I am not a Christian*, in which he stated that Jesus believed in eternal punishment and used fear, such as teaching about "the unpardonable sin" to scare people into conformity. He thought that teaching fear of eternal hell was a character flaw in Jesus, since a person with much compassion would not have taught such fearful doctrines.[2]

Many Christian preachers are of the opinion that a strong enough dose of eternal hell-fire preaching will frighten obstinate sinners into accepting Jesus as their Savior. This morbid emphasis on eternal hell fire terrorizes many Christians who are not obstinate sinners. They are good people doing their best to believe and live "right" but living in fear that their good will never be good enough.

Calvinists have a horribly negative message that only an "elect" few can be saved because the "elect" are the only ones God, for some inexplicable reason, has chosen to be saved. Billions of "unelect" people will be forever condemned to hell for no other reason than God simply did not elect them for salvation. It is very hard to believe that there are some intelligent, well-educated, well-meaning Christians who believe in Calvinism but, sadly, there are.

One such person was the late Dr. D. James Kennedy. Over thirty years ago I attended his evangelistic seminar called, "Evangelism Explosion," at his mega church in Florida. I talked with him then and on a subsequent occasion in New York. I have a letter from him confirming that he believed in Calvinism. He stated that, since we do not know who the elect are, we share the Gospel with all, knowing that only the elect will be saved.

These various versions of the Gospel are called good news. But what about the billions of people who have lived and died without ever hearing of salvation through Christ? What about

126

faithful adherents of other religions, children too young to understand, and adults who cannot understand due to being intellectually challenged? In this regard, the Gospel, as generally understood, is very "iffy," but God's promise is sure (Rom. 4:16).

Some Christians have asked me why I evangelize, since every one is going to be saved "anyway." I share the Good News in obedience to Christ's command to go into all the world and preach the Gospel. I was as faithful in sharing the Gospel as I was able to be while in active Christian ministry. Now that I am retired, I am active in sharing the Good News by preaching, teaching, writing books, and going into all the world via the Internet.

I have received emails, from across the USA and from around the world, informing me of how much victims of spiritual terrorism and spiritual insanity have been helped by reading my writings and visiting my website: HealingSpiritualTerrorism.com. Some of the countries from which I have received emails, in regard to *Spiritual Terrorism*, are: Australia, Canada, Germany, Great Britain, India, New Zealand, Poland, Saudi Arabia, and South Africa. Thus, I am still fulfilling The Great Commission from my home via modern technology, something the apostles could never have imagined but is a reality today.

Jewish Zionism

Jewish Zionism is the belief that Jews throughout the world should return to Israel, the land God gave to the descendants of Abraham. There they will flourish and make the desert blossom like a rose (Isaiah 35:1-4). Christian Zionists believe in the return of the Jews to Israel, from their dispersion throughout the world, but with a far different outcome. Dr. John Hagee, the literalist mentioned in the last chapter, is a devout Christian Zionist. He has raised millions of dollars for the cause of Jewish Zionism. What do Christian Zionists believe will happen to Israel after the return to their ancestral homeland? Israel will flourish, in spite of minor wars, until attacked by her enemies in the Battle of Armageddon (Rev. 16:16). Terrible end-time events are described in the

Revelation, chapters 8-19. Hundreds of millions, perhaps billions, of people worldwide will perish! A minority of Jews will be converted to Christianity and be saved, but most Jews will die.

I saw Jeremy Ben-Ami, a Jew who is the author of *A New Voice For Israel: Fighting For The Survival of The Jewish Nation*,[3] interviewed on TV. He said that he does not like this Christian version of the future of Israel, because it does not end well for Israel. That is a gross understatement! In this Christian scenario, the church will supplant Israel as the people of God. Per a literalist interpretation of the Revelation, Israel, as a Jewish state, will cease to exist, but *The Torah* proclaims that every knee shall bow and every tongue shall swear allegiance to the Lord. And all the descendants of Israel shall rejoice and glory (Isaiah 45:22-25). The New Testament proclaims the fulfillment of Isaiah's prophecy (Phil. 2:9-11) and specifically states that all Israel shall be saved (Rom. 11:26).

The Danger of Christian Zionism

Christian Zionists are 100 percent supporters of Israel, so what could be the danger of Christian Zionism? It could serve like a "Trojan Horse" in bringing about the destruction of Israel as a self-fulfilling prophecy. How so? In raising tens of millions of dollars and funneling it to the most extreme rightwing politicians in Israel, this could bring about the Battle of Armageddon, because Christian Zionists do not want Israel to compromise in the least with the Palestinians. Until there is justice for the displaced Palestinians, there will be no peace for Israel. The Israeli population appears to be much more willing to talk peace and even swap land with secure borders for peace, but this is not what the Christian Zionists want. They want Israel to have all the land, even beyond the 1967 borders approved by the United Nations. They believe that God gave the land to the Jews, and they must have every square foot of it. That would include the Sinai, Gaza, the West Bank, and Southern Lebanon. No compromise is what extreme right-wing politicians in Israel want.

In the Republican Primaries for President of the United States in 2012, the candidates were all in 100 percent support of Israel like good Christian Zionists. Newt Gingrich called the Palestinians an "invented people" and was absolutely opposed to any compromise. Michele Bachmann, Herman Cain, Rick Perry, Mitt Romney, and Rick Santorum, were equally opposed to compromise and expressed willingness and eagerness to bomb Iran in support of Israel. Comedian Jon Stewart, who is Jewish, said that the Republican candidates for president were all trying to impress the Jews as to who loved them more. The exception was Ron Paul who said that Israel should be treated equally as we treat other countries. All the other candidates dropped out of the race. Romney won the primaries and has been nominated as the presidential candidate. In his acceptance speech, at the Republican Convention, Romney appeared to be just as ready to bomb Iran. He mentioned Iran by name.

War hawks often fail to think of unintended consequences. If the United States should bomb Iran in defense of Israel, there could be such a backlash in the Islamic world that the radicals in Pakistan might be able to overthrow that unstable government, now our ally, and get their hands on nuclear weapons and nuke Israel from Pakistan, creating a disaster for both Israel and the USA [nuke Pakistan; consequences?]. The former head of Israeli Intelligence, Mossad, recently said on 60 Minutes that options other than war should be given a chance. He feared unintended consequences of bombing Iran. War always needs to be the last, not the first resort. Due to diplomatic and economic pressure from The U.S. and Europe, Iran has been meeting to discuss ending nuclear ambitions.

A New Voice for Israel

Jeremy Ben-Ami, author of *A New Voice For Israel,* and founder and president of J Street, a pro-Israel organization, sounded the alarm about Christian Zionism. He believes that if Israel is to survive as a Jewish nation, there must be a new, moderate voice speaking for Israel, rather than extremists. Ben-Ami made the following insightful statement.

Over the past two decades, perhaps the most important political alliance the American Jewish establishment has struck on behalf of Israel is with those Evangelical Christians known as Christian Zionists. And no single person has been more central to that friendship than Pastor John Hagee of San Antonio, Texas. Yet this alliance between the Jewish establishment and right-wing Christian Zionists turns off large numbers of mainstream Jewish Americans. They see their community sacrificing some of its core values and principles to ally with a group with whom we have little in common, simply to build a broader base of **unquestioning** support for Israel [bold mine].[4]

Ben-Ami said that since 1981, Ministries and Christians United for Israel (CUFI), founded by Hagee, have been "extremely lucrative," raising over 73 million dollars for Jewish and Israeli causes, 8.25 million in 2010. Hagee's right-wing religious stance:

This is the same John Hagee whose endorsement John McCain was forced to turn down in 2008 after a Hagee sermon came to light in which he portrayed Adolf Hitler as being sent by God to force 'Jews to come back to the land of Israel...' Hagee has been featured at major national Jewish organizational events...Senator Joe Lieberman has likened him to Moses...He's been greeted by the prime minister of Israel, Benjamin Netanyahu, who said, 'I salute you, the people of Israel salute you, the Jewish people salute you...' His organization brings over five thousand people at a time to lobby on Capitol Hill, where they greatly contribute to cementing the Israel-right-or-wrong grip on Congress and influence American policy toward the Middle East.[5]

I hasten to add that this is not just about John Hagee. He is only representative of the problem. Ben-Ami discussed several other Christian Zionists, none of whom have endorsed the two-state solution to the Israeli-Palestinian problem. The two-state solution is a Palestinian state living side-by-side in peace with the state of

Israel. This is my position, and I can think of nothing that would be more pleasing to God than for all of His children to live in peace with each other. That is why we are here on earth—to learn how to love and be loved and to forgive and be forgiven. We, as a human family, will eventually learn this lesson. The Jews and Palestinians could set the example for the world as to how we can achieve universal peace! Ben-Ami made this wise statement. "It is time to redefine what it means to be pro-Israel, to break out of the us-versus-them paradigm and to view support for the creation of a Palestinian state as a legitimately pro-Israel position, since without a Palestinian state living alongside Israel in peace and security, Israel cannot remain both Jewish and democratic."[6]

This is the same point made by various online sites which are pro-Israel. Unfortunately, Christian Zionists tend to label anyone who believes in a two-state solution as being anti-Israel. I am pro-Israel, but I agree with Ben-Ami—there will be no long-term peace for Israel without peace, security, and prosperity for the Palestinians. Understanding universal salvation will enable Christians to be both pro-Israeli and pro-Palestinian and be optimistic rather than fatalistic about the future! **Christians can thus be ambassadors of peace—not fear mongers—for Christ!**

Two of the Most Popular Evangelism Booklets

There are many negative, fear-mongering evangelism materials which have been published and used to "win [or scare] the world to Christ." Two of the most popular and positive evangelism booklets I have read are, respectively, *Do you know the steps to peace with God?* by Dr. Billy Graham, founder of the Billy Graham Evangelistic Association, and *HAVE YOU HEARD OF THE FOUR SPIRITUAL LAWS?* by the late Dr. Bill Bright, founder of Campus Crusade for Christ. Both booklets can be viewed online.

Tens of millions of these booklets have been printed and distributed. Step number two in both of these evangelistic tools says the problem with humanity is that people are sinful which separates them from God. Bright used the word "separated" twice while Graham used the word "separation" four times. The problem with both of these materials is they are based on the false premise that sinful mankind is separated from God and will be eternally separated from God if each and every sinner does not personally accept Christ as Savior and Lord in this life.

Why is this a false belief? According to *the Bible*, God is omnipresent. Therefore, no one can be separated from God for time or eternity. The Psalmist said to God, "Where shall I go from thy spirit? Or where shall I flee from thy presence? If I ascend up into heaven, thou art there: if I make my bed in hell [Sheol], behold, thou art there. If I take the wings of the morning and dwell in the uttermost parts of the sea: Even there shall thy hand lead me and thy right hand shall hold me" (Psalm 139:7-10).

So, therefore, sin causes mankind to be out of fellowship with God, but no one can be separated from God's presence, not even in hell. Timothy Ware, a Bishop in the Eastern Orthodox Church made this point in an extensive-profound statement on hell which I quoted in *Spiritual Terrorism* (chapter 23). Bishop Ware said that sinners in hell are not separated from the presence or love of God.[7]

He correctly stated it would be heretical to say that all must be saved, for that would deny free will, but it is orthodox to say that all may be saved. Ware also stated that many of the early church fathers believed all will eventually be saved. He pointed out that the great saint in the Eastern Church, Gregory of Nyssa, said that it is legitimate to even hope for the salvation of the Devil![8]

Dr. Robert L. Short, who wrote both *The Gospel According to Peanuts* (1964) and *The Parables of Peanuts (1968)*, is a retired Presbyterian minister who believes in CU. In *The Parables...*, Short stated that the Gospel is not both good news and bad news. It is just Good News.[9] After writing *Spiritual Terrorism*, I found out Dr. Short believes in CU so I called him and had a very stimulating conversation. He said Schultz, who wrote the "Peanuts Comic Script," also believed in CU and gave him permission to use "Peanuts" in his books.

Short shared with me that he made his confession of faith in Christ as a young man from the perspective of CU, and he initially assumed all Christians must believe in CU. He soon found out that very few Christians believe this wonderful truth of the Gospel.

Vulture Evangelism

Great harm has been and is being done to the cause of Christ's mission to destroy the works of the Devil and reconcile the world to God by Biblical literalists who "know" the end of the great redemptive story. These literalists teach that relatively few Christians will be saved while the masses of humanity will be tortured forever in literal hell fire. Clergy in mainline denominations tend to be better educated and have a better grasp on grace, so they allow for the possibility that God might eventually save every one, but they aren't sure of it. A Good example of this Biblical position is Rob Bell who wrote the book in 2011, *Love Wins: A Book About Heaven, Hell, and the Fate of Every Person Who Ever Lived,*[10] that was an instant best seller. Bell was the pastor of a ten-thousand-member Evangelical Church. Bell's book was published by HarperOne, which is a major publisher with the resources to advertise its products. It appears that a lot of money was spent on marketing. As soon as it was released, Evangelicals were in a frenzy calling Bell a heretic. Why? Because Bell stated the possibility that hell is not literal fire and that it could be for the purpose of purifying sinners, so every one will be saved.

Bell wisely stated that God is loving enough to save and reconcile all people to Himself. But he also stated that there is no assurance of it. Since love gives freedom, sinners can say "No" to God's love forever because love wins. Bell made the front cover of *Time Magazine,* and, in the interview, denied believing in universal salvation in any form. The ambiguity of making a good case for CU but denying belief in CU leaves many people living in uncertainty of salvation for themselves as well as loved ones. Martin Luther, in "Bondage of the Will" [on the Internet] called uncertainty "the most miserable thing in the world."[11]

People tend to prefer certainty (even if negative) to uncertainty. They are thus vulnerable to what Christian-Universalist, Dr. Short, called "**Vulture-Evangelists.**"[12] Short referred to Mark Twain who saw the humorous incongruity of Vulture-Evangelists who preached the "good news" of how beautiful heaven is and how nearly impossible it is to go there and how dreary hell is and how easy it is to go there. Vulture-Evangelists have proselytized millions of Christians from mainline Protestant Churches, "who only had 'head knowledge'" [had not personally accepted Jesus as Savior by praying "the sinner's prayer"], by getting them "saved" through fear of eternal torture in literal hell fire. The solution to this problem is for pastors to study diligently, be sure that *the Bible* teaches CU, and share the Good News with clarity, conviction, certainty, and courage speaking the truth in love (Eph 4:15).

Sound vs. Unsound Doctrine

A person contacted me expressing fear that CU is the unsound doctrine about which Paul warned Timothy. Paul said that the time would come when people will no longer endure sound doctrine (II Tim. 4:3). My response was that at the time the Apostle Paul penned this warning to young Timothy, in the first century, the sound doctrine was CU, and the unsound doctrine was eternal torture in hell fire. Jesus clearly taught CU, the apostles preached it, and the early church believed in CU for over 500 years. CU was not condemned as a heresy until Origen (185-254) was unjustly condemned in 553, **three centuries after his death!** Today, the fact most Christians believe in eternal hell fire is proof of what Paul foretold. Believing they know the truth, the minds of Biblical literalists are afraid to even listen to and weigh and consider the facts. President Reagan used to say, "Facts are stubborn things."

CU Both Implicit and Explicit

Universal salvation is implicit in the symbolism and explicit in the declarations: Christ drawing all to himself (John 12:32), all die in Adam/all live in Christ (I Cor. 15:22), God becoming "all in all" which means God being **everything to every one** (I Cor.

15:28 RSV), and worship of God and the Lamb is eternal (Rev. 5:13)! "Every created being" includes Satan and the fallen angels!

To help Christians share their faith from a totally positive perspective is why I developed the evangelistic booklet, *SALTED WITH FIRE: Five Liberating Truths—The Gospel in a Nutshell.* I plan to have it printed in booklet form and make it available to people who want to share the Gospel, which is ALL Good News!

Upon request, in its present form, it is being used by a Christian Church in South Africa. I will be glad to give permission to others.

Five Liberating Truths—The Gospel in a Nutshell

SALTED WITH FIRE

TRUTH #1: THE TRUTH WILL SET YOU FREE OF FEAR.

Jesus said that the truth shall set you free (John 8:32). The Biblical use of "fire" symbolizes purification. Thus, the word "fire" is used metaphorically. A metaphor is the use of a word meaning one thing to symbolize something else. For example:

Moses and the burning bush: fire did not burn the bush but purified—holy ground (Ex. 3:1-5). Messiah: will use a refining fire to purify the Jewish people (Mal. 3:1-3) and will baptize with the Holy Spirit and fire (Mt. 3:11). Pentecost: The Holy Spirit appeared as tongues of fire upon the apostles (Acts 2:1-3). The tongue: is a fire (Jas. 3:6). Fiery trials of life: modify behavior and refine people's character (I Pet. 4:12).

Interpreting fire literally is **spiritual abuse because it makes no sense** and frightens people, especially children, with the false doctrine of eternal punishment in hell fire for failure to obey "God's rules." Thus, this is **spiritual terrorism** the most extreme form of spiritual abuse. It is also spiritual insanity.

TRUTH #2: BELIEVERS WILL BE REFINED BY FIRE.

At the final judgment of believers, their works will be tested by fire, but they will be saved through the fire (I Cor 3:10-15). Salvation is a gift; a gift is free. For by grace you have been saved through faith; **the gift of God**, not according to works so that no person can boast (Eph. 2:8, 9). While salvation is a gift of grace, judgment, even for forgiven believers, is based on works (II Cor. 5:10). We cannot fool God; we reap as we have sown (Gal. 6:7).

The final judgment can best be understood by out-of-body death experiences; people report having a life review in which they see and feel the impact their lives have had on other people. **They feel like they are the other people.** What we dish out in life, good or bad, we will receive on Judgment Day! Thus, this fiery judgment is not to be feared but appreciated as God's perfect justice for all! Salvation is not a feeling but **knowing** you are saved (I John 5:13).

TRUTH #3: UNBELIEVERS WILL BE SALTED WITH FIRE.

Jesus, who was God in the flesh, explained the purpose of hell. He said, "For every one shall be salted with fire. . . " (Mk. 9:49). The **best translation** of this symbolic language—a mixed metaphor—of salt and fire, is found in *The Good News Bible: Today's English Version.* It says, **"Everyone will be purified by fire. . . ."** Every one in hell, **"salted with fire" are either the most horrifying or most loving words ever spoken!** This is evidence that demands a verdict.

It is spiritual abuse to say Jesus was only warning of a "terrible truth." This is not the truth at all. It is a terrible lie about our loving Lord! These are, indeed, the most loving words ever spoken! Even those in hell are not deprived of the love or presence of God, since God is omnipresent on land and sea and heaven and hell (Psalm 139:7, 8 KJV)! God loves all people—saints and unrepentant sinners—equally! God hates sin but loves sinners. God loves unbelievers in hell as much as believers in heaven!

God, who has infinite wisdom, knows how to destroy sin, not sinners, and, as a consuming fire (Deut. 4:24; Heb. 12:29), burns up sin which purifies sinners (Isa. 30:27-33). The door to hell is locked on the inside. After feeling the pain done to others, the "key" to unlock hell is willingly, humbly, and sincerely submitting to God's saving grace to the glory of God (Phil. 2:9-11).

TRUTH #4: SULFUR SYMBOLIZES PURIFICATION AND/OR HEALING.

The Revelation expresses this truth of purification by fire for unbelievers in another way—the lake of fire and brimstone. The definition of brimstone is "sulfur." This symbolism should be translated as **"the lake of burning sulfur"** which is how the *New International Version* of *the Bible* translated it (Rev. 20:10-15).

Sulfur was widely known in Biblical times as a multipurpose medication. A sulfur paste would cure a body sore. It was also burned in sulfur pots to disinfect homes after a person had died of an infectious disease. It was similarly burned to disinfest homes of lice, mice, and other vermin. People used sulfur to preserve produce. It was burned in religious settings to symbolize prayers of purification. Every way it was used had a beneficial meaning.

Sulfur symbolizes divine healing or being disinfected of sins. In Rev. 20, Hades/hell, death, and all spiritual rebels will be cast into the lake of burning sulfur. This is not God's cosmic torture chamber but recycling center or reform school (pigpen: Lk. 15:11-32)! Christ will draw all to himself (Jn. 12:32); all will live in Christ (I Cor. 15:22); and God will be all in all (I Cor. 15:28).

Universal worship is the eternal state (Rev. 5:13). The time in hell, the Greek words, "the aeons of the aeons" should be translated as "indefinitely," not as "forever and ever" (Rev. 20:10). All die in Adam; all live in Christ (I Cor. 15:22 and Rom. 5:10-21). With this Good News, all people can stop living in morbid fear of God and of death for themselves and "unsaved" loved ones. They will reverence God and be motivated for godly living, since no one can hurt others without hurting oneself. This creates **empathy**, feeling what others feel—**the most effective learning known to mankind**—God's method of behavior modification.

In the beginning, all were created in the image of God (Gen. 1:27). In many people God's image has been badly marred and scarred by sin. In some people God's image has been almost obliterated. But when sin, the spiritually combustible material, has been burned up, God's image will again shine brightly. **Thus, all will be purified, reconciled, and restored to God!!!**

TRUTH #5: ALL WILL WORSHIP GOD IN UNIVERSAL PEACE.

You can even overcome spiritual terrorism and spiritual insanity and find peace with God! You will be able to love God and your neighbor, enjoy peace of mind, and find power for living. Every one freely worshiping God is the eternal state (Rev. 5:13). Attending church preaching these truths will help spiritual growth.

C – hurch, a fellowship of believers where God is worshiped, The Gospel—Good News—preached, and Holy Communion is celebrated (Acts 2:41-47).

H – eaven assured as a gift of God's grace and mercy (Ephesians 2:8, 9; Tit. 3:5).

U – "U" are welcome, without exception, as children of God (James 2:1-18).

R – enew your mind with positive spiritual input (Romans 12:2; Phil. 4:6-9).

C – hrist, Messiah, is exalted as the Savior of the world (John 4:24-26, 42; I John 2:2).

H - ope for the world is to know The Savior and to hear The Good News of Christian Universalism: universal peace, purification, reconciliation, and restoration of all creation.

This is The Great Commission (Mt. 28:18-20). Be a peace maker, not a hell-fear monger. Come, help change the world as Christ's ambassadors of peace (II Corinthians 5:17-21).

Discussion Questions

1. What is the difference between an ambassador of peace and a fear monger for Christ?

2. If you have shared your Christian faith, what was your perspective? What would you like it to be?

3. Have you been taught and now believe that sinners can be forever separated from God? Based on Psalm 139:7, 8, is this possible? Why or why not?

4. Why will Christians need purifying by fire at the Judgment Seat of Christ, since salvation is by grace?

5. Until reading this book had you heard of being "salted with fire"? Can it be literal? What do you believe this mixed metaphor symbolizes? Why?

6. Have you been taught that sinners who are cast into the lake of fire and brimstone will be tormented day and night forever? Did you know that "brimstone is an outdated word for "sulfur"? Does it make sense that burning sulfur symbolizes purification and/or healing? Why or why not?

7. What is your assessment of "SALTED WITH FIRE: Five Liberating Truths—The Gospel in a Nutshell"?

8. What do you perceive the potential effectiveness to be of sharing one's faith via "SALTED WITH FIRE"? A pastor from a new Christian Church in South Africa emailed to ask for my permission to use this material. I gave it, and I will be looking forward to feedback on how effective it is.

9. Why, according to Dr. Robert Short, is the Gospel not both good news and bad news—just Good News?

Chapter 9
Nature, Science, and Medicine

The "N" in the acrostic, "CHRISTIANITY," represents "Nature, Science, and Medicine." Fundamental and Evangelical Christians are fond of saying people need to have a "Christian worldview." What is a Christian worldview, and how does it relate to Christian understanding of and stance on various issues in regard to nature, science, and medicine? Some have said a "Christian worldview" is a buzz or code word for the religious right's political agenda.

A Christian Worldview of Nature

Industry in our great country of the United States of America has a bad record of polluting our air, land, and water. I grew up in Northern Ohio, near Lake Erie, about 100 miles South West of Cleveland. Lake Erie was badly polluted by a great deal of industrial waste as well as other sources. And the Cuyahoga River in Cleveland, which emptied into Lake Erie, had a history of periodically catching on fire and burning until the fire department extinguished it [if you doubt this, Google it]. A river on fire—that is serious pollution from toxic chemicals!

Republican President Richard Nixon, who was certainly no "tree-hugging" liberal, supported and signed into law legislation founding the Environmental Protection Agency (EPA) to stop the pollution of our air, land, and water. On December 2, 2012, most Americans will celebrate while right-wing conservatives will lament the 40th anniversary of the EPA. Very conservative politicians have come to despise the EPA. They call it a "jobs-killing, out-of-control organization" and/or the "Employment Prevention Agency" which they want eliminated. Doubtlessly, it could stand some tweaking, but I, for one, would not want to go back to the bad old days when rivers caught on fire and the air in urban areas was so thick with pollutants that the joke was people trusted to breathe no air they could not see!

"Bible-believing Christians" tend to believe that Jesus is coming soon for His Second Advent so caring for the earth is not important. They contend that pollution doesn't matter, jobs are more important, global warming is a myth, there is nothing humans can do to affect the temperature and quality of life on earth, so there is no reason to conserve energy or increase mileage efficiency of vehicles. Their solution to our energy needs is simply "Drill, baby drill!" Even if we do drill here, drill there, and drill everywhere, the oil will not belong to the USA. It will belong to the multinational oil companies and it will be sold on the world market where China and India, two rapidly industrial developing countries, will be competing for this scarce and exhaustible energy supply. If our government approves building the potentially polluting XL Pipeline from Canada to refineries in Texas, the oil will belong to the Canadian oil company, not to the USA, so that oil will also be sold on the world market.

The main danger of pollution is to the Ogallala Aquifer the vast underground reservoir supplying fresh water for drinking and agriculture to Nebraska and seven other states in the region [a lot of info is on the Internet]. The soil of Nebraska, which is great for agriculture, is quite porous allowing storm water to easily seep down into and refill the aquifer. But the porous soil would also allow spilled oil to quickly seep down into and pollute the aquifer. Once polluted, how could this water underground ever be cleaned up? Environmentalists claim that the pipeline would in essence be a ticking time bomb due to breaks in hundreds of miles of pipeline, due to accidents, corrosion, earthquakes, etc. Which is more important, oil or drinking water? What is a Christian worldview on this issue? How about Jesus' teaching—the Golden Rule—"Do unto others as you would have them to do unto you" (Mt. 7:12)?

Since President Obama delayed approval of the construction of the XL Pipeline, due to pollution concerns, the Canadian oil company has proposed rerouting the pipeline. It thus would not take the shortest route diagonally across the Sandhills region of Nebraska, which is especially environmentally sensitive to polluting the Ogallala Aquifer. The alternative proposed route would be better, but it would still cross the aquifer. The pipeline may have to take a longer detour to miss the aquifer completely in order to get final approval from the Federal Government.

China has 1.3 billion people, a billion more than we have. And India has almost a billion. As these potential economic giants develop, there will be fierce competition for energy which, with intermittent dips, will keep the price of oil and gasoline high. Cars fueled by electricity or natural gas [abundant in the USA] or electric/natural gas hybrid vehicles could serve us well.

My mother was a very wise woman who always said, "An ounce of prevention is worth a pound of cure." That being true, just in case global warming is not a myth, wouldn't it be wise to go green for the good of our planet, our health, and our lives? Even if it cost us more, would it not be better to develop natural gas, solar, wind, hydro, tides, geothermal, and ethanol [from sugar cane/saw grass/algae—non-food] sources of energy which would give us a healthier environment and make us independent of OPEC— Organization of Petroleum Exporting Countries—and create millions of well-paying jobs in America?

According to Internet research on alternative energy, the earth receives an incredible supply of solar energy every minute of every hour of every day 24/7, since the sun is always shining on one side of the earth. The earth receives enough energy from the sun in one minute to supply the world's present energy needs for one year! It provides enough energy in one day to supply the energy needs of earth's current population for 27 years! And in a three-day period the amount of energy from the sun is equal to all the energy stored in all fossil-energy sources including coal, natural gas, and oil in the whole world! China is hugely investing in solar cells, which will probably power the long-term future. Mass production will greatly reduce costs. When first marketed, VCRs, for example, cost about $1,500, but, by the time they were replaced by DVDs, they cost less than $100. Should the failure of Solyndra stop all government promotion of solar research and development? What is a Christian worldview of energy?

A Christian Worldview of Creation

Even when God said, "Let there be light," it may well have been an extremely complex happening. A math teacher shared with me what peace of mind she now has, from reading *Spiritual Terrorism*, in regard to the assurance of the salvation of her late father who was a good man but not a Christian. This same teacher bought me a T-shirt she saw at a math conference. Printed on the T-shirt are the words "God Said: [followed by a long mathematical equation depicting how the light may have been created] And There Was Light." God may well have put a lot of engineering technology into the creation of the universe. Einstein said that God did not play dice with the cosmos.

It is significant that the first thing God created was light (Gen. 1:3). According to scientists, everything in the universe, from rocks and trees, skies and seas, all living things, including humans, is simply a different density of light! Light has no aging process; there is no new light or old light—light is light. And if people could travel at the speed of light (186,000 miles per second), no one would ever age. One of the four Biblical definitions of God is, "God is light" (I John 1:5); we, in this sense, are made of God.

According to the creation account, "And the Lord God formed man of the dust of the ground, and breathed into his nostrils the breath of life; and he became a living soul" (Gen. 2:7). Readers, do you believe God literally knelt on the ground and, with His hands, sculpted Adam out of the dust? God, who is Spirit (John 4:24), literally has no knees on which to kneel and no hands with which to sculpt. Do you believe God literally performed CPR on Adam by putting His mouth [which God does not literally have] on Adam's nose composed of dust, and breathed into his nostrils [of which there would have been, as yet, no air passageway] the breath of life? And this is, literally, how Adam became a living human being?

All of this is a case of anthropomorphism—ascribing human characteristics to God or inanimate things. Literalism defies logic!

The brilliant theoretical physicist, Stephen Hawking, at Cambridge University, in Great Britain, in 1998, wrote the book, *A Brief History of Time*. I have "The Updated and Expanded Tenth Anniversary Edition" in which Hawking addressed the place of God in the origin of the universe. He made this profoundly insightful statement which has great implications for people to be able to believe in God and science, not God or science. "The idea that space and time may form a closed surface without boundary also has profound implications for the role of God in the affairs of the universe. With the success of scientific theories in describing events, most people have come to believe that God allows the universe to evolve according to a set of laws and does not intervene in the universe to break these laws. However, the laws do not tell us what the universe should have looked like when it started—it would still be up to God to wind up the clockwork and choose how to start it off. So long as the universe had a beginning, we could suppose it had a creator."[1]

Hawking, however, went on to say, "But if the universe is really completely self-contained, having no boundary or edge, it would have neither beginning nor end; it would simply be. What place, then, for a creator?" So, readers, there you have it, the case for or against believing in God. This is exactly what I have long contended; it is equally a matter of faith to believe or not believe in the existence of God. Whether people believe in God or not, simply boils down to a matter of faith. I contend it takes more faith to believe the universe has always been or came from nothing, and everything is a cosmic and/or biological accident, than to believe God has always been and created everything in the visible universe. I believe the latter. What about you?[2]

A Christian Worldview of Science

The worldview of politically right-wing Christians is that, *the Bible* is the infallible word of God in all areas of life including science. There is, of course, the long-standing controversy over Darwinian evolution going back to the "Scopes 'Monkey' Trial" in Dayton, Tennessee, in 1925. A public school science teacher, John

Scopes, was charged with violating the state law against teaching evolution. The state won the case, but the case was overturned on a technicality. Scopes went free, and seems to have won in the court of academic freedom.

But the theological controversy still rages today almost a century after the Scopes Trial ended. Many efforts have been made by "Bible-believing Christians" to ban the teaching of evolution in public schools or to teach creation science along with evolution. Efforts have failed to ban the teaching of evolution, but there has been some success in getting creation science included in school curriculum. Evolutionary scientists tend to call "creation science" an oxymoron. Creationists call evolution unbiblical and anti-God. Some "Bible-believing" parents have decided to pay the price to have their children educated in a Christian school so they can be taught science based on *the Bible*.

Those who believe in a literal understanding of the six-day creation story and the genealogical records in *the Bible* contend that planet earth is only about 5,000 years old. The vast majority of scientists believe that our earth is at least four billion years old, and the universe, as we can observe it, is at least 15 billion years old. An excellent book on cosmological science is *The Universe in a Nutshell*[3] authored by Stephen Hawking who is Professor of Mathematics at the University of Cambridge. He is highly regarded as one of the most brilliant theoretical physicists since Einstein.

Is there actually a conflict between what *the Bible* says and what modern scientists teach? Would it not resolve the apparent problem by simply believing what *the Bible* says in the first verse of the first chapter of the first book of *the Bible*? "In the beginning God created the heavens and the earth." That is certainly all I need to know and believe. *The Bible* is not a science book and says nothing about a multitude of scientific issues, such as: general relativity, quantum physics and mechanics, 10-dimensional membranes, 11-dimensional super gravity, string theory, parallel universes, dark holes, etc.

It is theorized that everything which can be observed in the universe was, in the beginning, super compacted into a molecule of incredible density, of immense weight which was no bigger than a virus and then exploded and has continued to expand into the mind-boggling vastness we see today. All plant, animal, and human life just happened spontaneously or was pre-programmed into the cosmos.

Assuming what scientists generally believe is true, does it eliminate God or in the least minimize the greatness of God? For me, it only increases the wonderment, the grandeur, and awe of God and the miracle of creation! Such a fantastic conception of God does not destroy or even diminish my faith in God. Conversely, it really moves me to exclaim, in the words of the great hymn, "My God, How Great Thou Art!"

A Christian Worldview of Medicine

There are various aspects in regarding medical care that may involve subtle spiritual abuse. It may not be thought of as such, but it is spiritually abusive, nevertheless, for parents "of faith" to refuse standard (not experimental) medical care for their children. Such parents may have prayed for their children and were trusting God to heal them of cancer or other life-threatening illnesses. Should parents have the right to refuse standard medical care for their children as well as themselves?

For example, blood transfusions have saved millions of lives, but Jehovah's Witnesses do not believe in blood transfusions due to *the Bible* saying that the life of the flesh is in the blood to make atonement for people's souls (Lev. 17:11). As a lifelong blood donor, it is tragic to realize that even when there is an ample supply of blood, some religious people refuse a needed blood transfusion for themselves and even for their children, because they have been taught and believe that it is against God's will.

146

Some parents, on religious grounds, have refused to have their children immunized against serious or even deadly diseases. Yes, some parents may object based on the fear of potential medical harm as a result of the vaccine. But, based solely on religious grounds, it is a needless tragedy when children get gravely ill, are handicapped for life, or even die because they have not been immunized against common diseases! To prevent such senseless tragedies, states have passed laws to prohibit parents, on religious grounds, from denying their children immunizations, blood transfusions, and other standard medical treatments. This problem of refusal of medical care, based on religious beliefs, is addressed in the comprehensive *Handbook of Religion and Health*.[4] Such understanding and refusal of child care is child abuse due to spiritual insanity.

Other people, based on religious convictions, may seek medical treatment but delay doing so in a timely manner until cancer has spread or another life-threatening illness has become inoperable or untreatable. Delay may have been due to seeking healing from a faith healer. The religious faith of the vast majority of people allows them to pray to God for healing and, at the same time, seek medical treatment. But some "faith healers" preach that it shows a lack of faith in God if those who are sick seek medical treatment.

Praying and Asking in Jesus' Name

Some have a "name-it and claim-it" theology, which means that true believers just need to name the healing they want and claim it in Jesus' name and be healed. Diabetics have thus started acting like they have been healed by stopping their medication and have gone into insulin shock or coma, and some have died due to this kind of "faith healing"—blind faith and spiritual insanity.

Dr. Rocco Errico explained, in the Aramaic Language which Jesus spoke, the meaning of praying and asking in Jesus' name as He instructed His followers to do. Errico said it is not a magic formula by which one simply says the words "in Jesus' name" and what one desires miraculously happens.

He used this example: Einstein split the atom with a very precise mathematical formula. If a very well-meaning believer in Einstein were to say to an atom, "Atom, split in the name of Einstein!" do you think the atom would split? Not a chance! But when scientists today use Einstein's formula, the atom splits. "In the name of Jesus" means to live like Jesus lived, love how Jesus loved, and give of oneself as Jesus gave of Himself. Thus, healing may be through the formula of modern medicine.[5]

Blood and Tissue Donations

While relatively few people give blood, even fewer are organ donors. Many potential donors die and no one in need of an organ benefits because of misinformation or lack of information. It may also be due to personal, moral, or religious convictions that it is wrong to donate blood and/or organs. What would please God more than for people to help our brothers and sisters in the human family (here and around the world) regardless of race, religion, ethnic origin, sex, sexual orientation, or any other factor?

I have been an organ donor for over 40 years, and it is so designated on my driver's license. To insure that my desire to help others is carried out, I have had a living will for almost 40 years. When a law was passed that made it possible to legally appoint a medical power of attorney (MPOA), I did so. It is important to complete both documents and to keep information updated. Some states now have e-directories, as West Virginia does [877-209-8086; fax 304-293-7442], making patients' desires immediately available to professionals providing medical care.

Living Wills and Medical Power of Attorney

The spiritual aspect of medical ethics is a topic that I covered in the hospice volunteer training programs which were conducted twice a year. All new staff members must also attend this training program. Volunteers as well as staff, patients, caregivers, and other family members need to be knowledgeable about medical ethics in regard to spirituality. The hospice social workers help patients or caregivers (for patients who are not able to do so) complete a living will and MPOA. Hospice does nothing to hasten a patient's death, but neither does hospice do anything to prolong the natural process of dying.

People who are not hospice patients and still in good health should have a living will and MPOA for stating their desires for or refusal of medical treatment. Some people are afraid to have a living will because they, mistakenly, believe that everything heroic to save their lives might not be done. It is important to have a living will whether people's desire is to have everything possible done as long as possible to save their lives. It is just as important to have a living will and MPOA for refusal of certain medical treatments such as resuscitation, feeding tubes, and artificial life support. They also need to be kept updated.

When asked, almost all elderly people say they would like to die at home. The sad reality, though, is the majority of people die in a hospital. People want and emotionally need "high touch" at home at the end of life; what they usually get is "high tech" in a hospital. Dying peacefully at home has been what people have done for thousands of generations and still do in most countries of the world. People died at home, with their extended family by their bedside, and their funerals were conducted at home.

Now, in the United States, we have hospitals and nursing homes where most people die, and their funerals are conducted in funeral homes. Thus, dying can be very expensive and impersonal. According to online research, 40 percent of Medicare spending is for medical care for patients in the last 30 days of life. The life savings of some people may be consumed in end-of-life care in nursing homes, since it is not covered by Medicare.

A Christian Worldview of End-of-Life Care

The elderly die peaceful deaths if they are given proper medications, including necessary pain relievers, and there is no interference with the natural dying process. The medical director of hospice has explained, in our patient-care meetings, that when patients can no longer eat and drink, within a week their kidneys shut down, uric acid builds up in the blood, and they experience a completely painless death. This apparently is God's design for no pain and suffering at the end of life. To call 911, rush patients at the end of life to a hospital, do CPR and electrically shock, insert an IV for hydration and a tube for feeding, and put the patients on a ventilator is a cruel, not a loving, thing to do. It is something done to patients—not something done for them. God certainly does not require unnecessary, unnatural, unloving, and extraordinary means of prolonging the dying process.

In over 14 years of conducting hospice volunteer training programs, I have had clergy from a broad spectrum of Christianity—Anglicans, Catholics, Orthodox, and various Protestants [as well as clergy of other religions]—to present their views on spirituality and dying. Everyone has stated that nothing must be done to shorten or take lives; and comfort measures must be given. But in regard to medical care for end-of-life treatment, not one religious representative has ever said God requires everything that can be done medically must be done to dying patients. To teach that God does require extraordinary means of medical treatment at the end of life is spiritual insanity.

Hard Choices for Loving People

For those readers who are presently caring for loved ones who are dying and those who will be caring for dying loved ones, I strongly recommend a booklet authored by Chaplain Hank Dunn, *Hard Choices for Loving People*.[6] It explains in much greater detail what I have shared with you. With the Baby-Boomer Generation starting to turn 65, in the near future tens of millions of families will soon be facing hard choices in the care of their loved ones. Dunn's booklet, first published in 1990, has sold over a million copies and is regularly updated. He is a hospice and nursing home chaplain who conducted a seminar which I attended. The seminar was excellent, and so is the booklet which also deals with various spiritual issues often involved in the end-of-life care.

Playing God

Some religious people say that it is "playing God" if family members want to remove medical life-support equipment. Such a case that will have long-term ramifications in health care is that of Terri Schiavo [often seen spelled in the media and on the Internet as "Shivo"]. Terri was 26 years old when in 1990 she suddenly stopped breathing and was rushed to the hospital. Her breathing was restarted, but her brain, according to news reports, had been starved of oxygen for 14 minutes causing irreversible brain damage. According to some medical reports, Terri was brain dead which has become the generally accepted definition of death.

Terri's husband, Michael, contended that she was brain dead and should be taken off life support. But her parents and brother and sister, citing other medical reports, contended that she was still alive and should be kept on life support. Terri's family and Michael saw things entirely differently religiously, ethically, and medically. Both sides went to court in seeking justice for Terri.

In the next seven years there were 14 appeals as well as many hearings, motions, and petitions in the Florida state courts. There were five federal court decisions. Florida state legislation, "Terri's Law," to keep her alive, was struck down as unconstitutional by the U. S. Supreme Court. A congressional committee issued a subpoena to give Terri "witness protection." The U. S. Congress passed legislation to give the right to life advocates access to federal courts, since this had been a state issue. The U. S. Supreme Court four times declined to hear appeals. The Pope and President George W. Bush made appeals to save Terri's life. The final court decision came on March 18th ordering the removal of Terri's feeding tube. She was officially pronounced dead March 31, 2005.

Ramifications

All the principals in the case were Roman Catholic, so it pitted Catholic against Catholic and Michael Schiavo against his church. After Terri's death, the Pope narrowed the cope of reasons for which a feeding tube could be removed. According to news reports, the public was overwhelmingly in support of the right to die, saying that they would not want to be kept alive under such circumstances. This sparked a national debate on the ethical, moral, and spiritual issues regarding end-of-life care. Ethics committees wrestled with the issues involved in this case. Many people sought information on living wills and medical powers of attorney.

The key lesson to be learned from this case is that whether people are for or against certain medical treatments, they need to have a living will and medical power of attorney. If people of whatever persuasion do not have the foresight to put in writing their desires for end-of-life care and appoint a MPOA others will be making those decisions for them. Those left to make crucial, life and death decisions may be people whose personal, ethical, political, and religious convictions are at odds with those of the patients. It is important for young people to make such designations too and to keep them updated.

A Christian Worldview of Stem-Cell Research

The Catholic Church and other conservative churches are opposed to embryonic stem-cell research. Many medical doctors believe the future of modern medicine is based on stem-cell research—adult, if not embryonic. I have a cartoon by Rogers, in the Sunday Gazette-Mail Newspaper, on May 29, 2005, in which a preacher, in the pulpit, says, "Let's pray for those sinners who engage in the Devil's work of stem-cell research!" This cartoon also shows three congregants sitting in a pew, with their hands folded, praying [thought-bubble above each bowed head], "Lord, help them find a cure for Dad's Alzheimer's…, A cure for Mom's Parkinson's…A cure for my cancer…." Readers, do you believe God will answer their prayers by a miraculous healing or through modern medicine—perhaps through stem-cell research, the very thing many Christian Churches are preaching against?

A Personhood Constitutional Amendment

I believe in the sanctity of human life. When, however, is opposing abortion going too far? It is in trying to get a "Personhood Amendment" added to the constitution. As proposed, a personhood amendment would define life as beginning at conception. Therefore, there would be no exception for abortion in the case of rape or incest, the health of the mother, **or even the life of the mother!** A Denver-based anti-abortion group, Personhood USA, has twice tried and failed to get a personhood amendment passed in Colorado. That is one of the least likely states in which to get such legislation passed, since Colorado is one of the states most likely to expand, not restrict, civil rights. It was the first state in the union to ratify the 19th Amendment to the U.S. Constitution giving women the right to vote. In 2011 Personhood USA tried to get a personhood amendment passed in Mississippi, the reddest of the politically red states. It was defeated by about 60 percent. Now, Personhood USA has announced that they are going to try it again in 2012 in Colorado, Montana, and Oregon.

The reason it will most likely be defeated again is that it is too extreme. Such an amendment would prohibit childless couples from having invitro fertilization. This is because multiple eggs are fertilized, and only the most viable ones are implanted into the woman's uterus. Personhood advocates thus claim that this procedure to enable women to have children is actually killing children due to fertilized eggs dying. Even worse, a personhood amendment would be a death sentence for a woman who has the misfortune to have a tubal pregnancy. Normally an egg is fertilized in the fallopian tube, descends from the tube, and implants on the uterine wall where it grows to full term. But at times, the fertilized egg does not exit the fallopian tube and begins developing in the tube. As the fetus grows, it causes excruciating pain for the woman. This anomaly will lead to her death unless her fallopian tube is surgically removed. But personhood advocates contend that this procedure kills the baby although the fetus would die anyway along with the mother. Ethically, surgically removing the fallopian tube would be doing the greater good of saving the mother's life.

Over a quarter century ago when I was the pastor of an Evangelical Church, a very well educated woman and man, in their late thirties got married. They wanted to have children, and she was able to get pregnant the first year of marriage. She, however, had an ectopic pregnancy and was in intense pain. Her husband rushed her to the hospital where the doctor surgically removed her fallopian tube with the fetus. I was not asked for my opinion before the fact, but later I expressed my support that she and her husband had made a very wise, though painful, decision which would be pleasing to our loving Lord. She still wanted to be a mother, but, at her age and with only one fallopian tube, her chances were significantly diminished. She, fortunately, was able to get pregnant and gave birth to a healthy child. She was able to conceive twice again and had two more healthy children. This lady, a school teacher, has been a loving-devoted mother, and her children, whom she home schooled, are now in college or are graduates.

But had there been a personhood amendment codified into law, this woman would have been dead as a result of her first pregnancy! The rest of this wonderful story of late-in-life motherhood would never have happened. Readers, what do you believe, and where do you stand on this issue? If such a personhood amendment is put on the ballot in your state, will you vote for or against it? Almost all people are opposed to the government coming between patients and their doctors. But religious conservatives on these vital—even life-and-death—issues want the government to make health-care decisions for women. "Personhood" is a plank in the 2012 Republican platform.

Women readers, do you believe that God, who is love, would expect you to sacrifice your life if you had a tubal pregnancy? If so, would you, especially if you already had children? Almost all mothers want nothing more than to live long enough to be able to get their children reared to adulthood. If some women would give up their life, should the law mandate it for all mothers in this situation? In the 2012 presidential campaign, some have called various legislative bills controlling women's health, "a war on women." To codify religious beliefs into law is spiritual insanity!

A generation ago, Dr. Francis Schaeffer was the "philosopher-in-chief" for the Evangelical movement in America. Though Schaeffer was an American, he had his home and international retreat center, L'Abri, in Switzerland. Dr. Schaeffer was a widely read author. He also did a film series, "How Should We Then Live?" It was viewed and discussed in many Evangelical Churches, one of which was the church I was pastoring. The message was about living a Christian life and making a difference in the modern world. Dr. Schaeffer is now deceased, but his son, Frank [then called "Frankie"] Schaeffer, has written a "tell-all" book about Dr. Schaeffer and their family. The title is *Crazy for God: How I Grew up as one of the Elect, Helped Found the Religious Right, and Lived to Take All (or Almost All) of it Back.*[7]

Frank shared that at the height of his father's ministry, abortion was not an issue for Evangelical Christians. His father considered it to be a Roman Catholic issue. But Frank related that he was instrumental in getting his famous father to take up the issue of abortion and get conservative Christians to rally to the cause. In some instances Evangelicals became even more radical and activist in battling abortion than Catholics. Later, when Frank became convinced that Evangelicals had become too radical on this issue, he spoke out against radicalism.

Until then, Frank was widely sought as the principal speaker everywhere in the Evangelical world. He was the poster boy for the cause. After that, Frank was no longer wanted as a speaker on the Evangelical-speaking circuit. He later left the Evangelical movement and became a member of the Eastern Orthodox Church where he now has his membership. Today, Frank, like more and more Evangelicals, is not a one-issue voter. Many Evangelicals believe there are other significant issues in the world—environmental issues such as air and water pollution and global warming; overpopulation; social justice issues of feeding the hungry and helping the poor; nuclear non-proliferation and disarmament, etc. Republicans tend to be strong on banning abortion but weak on environmental issues and social justice. Democrats tend to be pro-choice but strong on the environment and social justice. What would be a "Christian worldview"? Could Christians vote Democratic or Republican and be okay with God? By way of self disclosure, I am a registered Independent voter.

Discussion Questions

1. When you can no longer make medical decisions for yourself, would you rather receive treatment according to your desires or other people's desires?

2. What is your Christian worldview?

3 Do you believe that the world is going to end soon? If so, how important is protecting the environment?

4. Is evolutionary science destructive to your faith? Why?

5. From a Biblical perspective, what does it mean for mankind to have dominion and care of the earth?

6. Should "Bible-believing Christians" and all people have a reverent attitude for mother earth which sustains all forms of life on this planet? Explain.

7. What should be the Christian worldview on the role of the government in women's health regarding birth control for family planning and other health issues?

8. Are you for or against a personhood amendment to he Constitution of the Federal Government or to the constitution of your state? Why or why not? Could there be a better example of the government coming between a woman and her doctor?

Chapter 10
Inescapable Love of God

The third "I" in the acrostic, "CHRISTIANITY," represents the "Inescapable Love of God," as well as irresistible grace and infinite mercy. Christians read, talk, and sing about God's great love, grace, and mercy, but there is a big problem. With few exceptions, they do not believe what they read, say, and sing. There is no better example of that than this great song written by Frederick Lehman (1868-1953) in 1917. The lyrics are based on the Jewish poem, *Haddamut*, written in Aramaic in 1050 by Meir Ben Isaac Nehorai. It has been translated into at least 18 languages. Here are 12 of 28 lines on the amazing love of God!

The Love of God

> The love of God is greater far
> Than tongue or pen can ever tell
> It goes beyond the highest star
> And reaches to the lowest hell.
>
> Could we with ink the ocean fill
> And were the skies of parchment made
> And were every stalk on earth a quill
> And every man a scribe by trade
>
> To write the love of God above
> Would drain the ocean dry
> Nor could the scroll contain the whole
> Though stretched from sky to sky.

Wow! What great words expressing such wonderful theology! It is such a shame that so few Christians believe in this much love, as evidenced by their "turn-or-burn" belief in hell. You could write about all the love of God in which most Christians believe with only one ballpoint pen and still have most of the ink left over!

Nehorai may well have believed in this much love. But I wonder if Lehman believed what he wrote, since he was a Nazarene. The Church of the Nazarene is an Evangelical denomination which holds, as a tenet of the Christian faith, belief in the doctrine of eternal punishment. There are Nazarenes, as there are believers in other conservative denominations, who do believe in Christian Universalism.

After coming to believe in CU almost a quarter of a century ago, I talked with the pastor of a large Nazarene Church who impressed me as having a loving heart and an open mind. When I had shared the results of my diligent study of *the Bible*, including the Greek text with him, this was his compassionate response. "I don't have a problem with your theology, but tell me this, how long will unrepentant sinners be in hell?" I replied, "That is an excellent question, and I will be glad to answer it for you if you will first answer a question for me. He said, "What's that?' I responded, "In Jesus' Parable of the Prodigal Son, how long was the son in the pigpen feeding swine?"

He evidenced a good knowledge of Jesus' parable when he rather quickly said, "He was there, according to Jesus, until he came to his senses." I said, "That is exactly how long unrepentant sinners will be in hell, the cosmic pigsty. This parable is a microcosm of God and the human race. When they have felt the pain they have inflicted on others, and felt the privation of being out of fellowship with God, they will come to their senses resulting in every knee humbly bowing and every tongue sincerely confessing Jesus as Lord to the glory of God" (Phil. 2:9-11).

There are several renditions of "The Love of God" on the Internet. I counted at least ten pages with ten entries per page. There is a video with only piano music and the words of several different languages visually displayed. There is one of guitar-only music. There is one with introductory preaching by a young Billy Graham, and then people enthusiastically singing this song, with hands raised, glorifying God for such great love, "...**which shall evermore endure.**" It is obvious that Dr. Graham does not believe in this much love of God due to the fact that he has all of his long-ministerial life preached the doctrine of eternal punishment in hell.

As I did this Internet search, I wondered if any of the singers actually believed what they were singing. This much love would absolutely preclude belief in eternal torture. Bill Gaither wrote a similar song, with his modification to the unlimited love of God.

The Love of God

The love of God has been extended
To a fallen race
Through Christ the Savior of all men...
[it goes on to say]:
It goes beneath the deepest stain
That sin could ever leave
Redeeming souls to live again
Who will on Christ believe....

So this super-abundant, unbounded, unlimited love of God is limited to those who hear the Christian message of salvation in Christ and personally accept Jesus as their Savior in this life only. This song has 24 lines, six verses with four lines each. The above are just seven lines which tell the story of the adaptation of Lehman's inspiring song of God's unlimited love. Is it not oxymoronic to say that "Christ is the Savior of all men" and that the love of God "goes beneath the deepest stain that sin could ever leave, redeeming souls to live again..." and not conclude God will eventually save every created being in the whole world? While it is for all sinners, "who will on Christ believe," why put a time limit on it of this life only? Jesus did not, and *the Holy Bible* surely doesn't. But what about Hebrews 9:27?

Eternal "damnationists" usually cite Hebrews 9:27 which says that it is appointed unto mankind once to die, but after that is the judgment. But this verse says nothing about hell, the nature of hell, nor how long sinners may be sentenced to hell. God's

159

judgment will be fair, and the sentence will be for the purpose of purifying sinners and reconciling and restoring them to fellowship with God. To put God "in a box," by time-limiting salvation, while teaching that God's love is unconditional and everlasting, is what I called in *Spiritual Terrorism*, "Spiritual Schizophrenia." Another very appropriate term for this split mindset, in regard to the love of God, is "Spiritual Insanity!"

The Inescapable Love of God

Dr. Thomas Talbott wrote an excellent book with a great title, *The Inescapable Love of God.*[1] Dr. Talbott is a retired professor of Religion and Philosophy at Willamette University in Salem, Oregon. He grew up in conservative Christian Churches that preached the doctrine of eternal damnation in hell fire. He shared his struggle in coming to the Biblical truth of Christian Universalism. After reading this outstanding book, I wrote a five-star review of it and posted it on Amazon.com.

"The Inescapable Love of God is a terrific book. The title is terrific because it captures the wonderful Biblical concept of irresistible grace by which God, without violating anyone's free will, shall ultimately destroy evil and reconcile the whole cosmos to Himself. Dr. Talbott has a very understandable writing style. It is evident that he has extensive knowledge of *the Bible*, theology, and philosophy, and expresses it in a clear, concise, and gentle way. He has done an outstanding job of researching and condensing church history to give readers a brief, yet rather thorough, understanding of the theology of the early church. He carefully explains how and where it went wrong in turning from the glorious doctrine of universal salvation in Christ to the salvation of relatively few and the eternal damnation of the vast majority of the human race in literal hell fire. This ungodly and inhumane false doctrine is what I have called 'spiritual terrorism.' An analogous term is 'spiritual insanity!'"

"Dr. Talbott insightfully addressed the profoundly negative impact Augustine has had, theologically, on the Christian Church in the West. He also addressed the horrific spiritual devastation Emperor Justinian, of the Roman Empire, has had on the Western church. This is evident by the condemnation and persecution of Christians who believed in universal reconciliation and the commendation and elevation of Christian leaders who advocated eternal damnation. He rightly contends that the love-based Christianity was thus reduced to fear-based religion which was used as a means of social control to keep the subjects of the Roman Empire in subjection. Dr. Talbott wisely stated the horrendous tragedy this has been. Consequently, the Christian Church lost its spiritual and moral authority!"[2]

In regard to the false doctrine of eternal damnation, Dr. Talbott stated, "If supreme power lies on the side of supreme love, then none of us, whether Christian, Muslim, or even atheist, need fear that the One who loved us into existence in the first place might wantonly abandon us in the end. Nor need we worry that an honest mistake in theology will somehow jeopardize our future."[3] Certainly, God will not abandon anyone at all, much less forever.

"Not even one created being will be forever left behind. What a terrific conception of THE SUPREME BEING—SUPREME POWER on the side of SUPREME LOVE! Thus, God cannot fail to destroy the works of the Devil and reconcile the whole universe to God's self! This book is richly deserving of a five-star rating."

The New Revised Standard Version of the Holy Bible is a very good translation in several ways. One of these ways is that the NRSV translated Acts 3:21, which the KJV translated as the "restoration of all things," as the time of "universal restoration." It translated Rev. 20:10 not as the lake of fire and brimstone [the outdated word for "sulfur"] but as the lake of fire and sulfur.

The NRSV also has helpful chapter headings. The heading for Psalm 139 is "The Inescapable God." This Psalm specifically states that there is no place on land or sea or heaven or hell [KJV] (Sheol, Hebrew word for the grave or abode of the dead) where one can go from God's presence. Since God is love and is omnipresent, no one can ever be out of God's presence nor be absent from God's love for a moment, much less for eternity!

Irresistible Grace

The theological term I used in *Spiritual Terrorism* for the inescapability of God's saving grace is "irresistible grace." Irresistible grace is a key component of Calvinism, but it is a valid concept in historic Christianity. It is what Jesus taught, the apostles preached, and the early church believed. It needs to be applied to every created being, not to just a Calvinistic "elect" few. It is synonymous with the term "inescapable love of God."

In 2011, Rob Bell's *Love Wins: A Book About Heaven, Hell, and the Fate of Every Person Who Ever Lived,*[4] was an instant best seller. Bell was the pastor of a ten-thousand-member Evangelical Church. Bell's book was published by HarperOne, which is a major publisher with the resources to advertise its products. It appears that a lot of money was spent on marketing. As soon as it was released, Evangelicals were in a frenzy calling Bell a heretic. Why? Because Bell stated the possibility that hell is not literal fire and that it could be for the purpose of purifying sinners, so every one will eventually be saved.

Consequently, there is the possibility that God will eventually, without violating sinners' free will, reconcile and restore all sinners to God's self. Bell did not say for sure that God will do that, but he clearly made a good case that God might do so. If universal salvation never happens, it will be because sinners in hell forever resist God's saving grace. As a result of the popularity of *Love Wins*, Bell made the cover of *Time Magazine*. In the interview, he denied being a Universalist and denied believing in universalism in any form. I wrote a review of *Love Wins* and posted it on Amazon.com, the essence of which is shared below:

"The book *Love Wins*, by Rob Bell, is an excellent fresh examination of the Christian faith. This author examines Christianity from an Evangelical perspective, and asks

many thought-provoking questions in regard to whether what Christians in general, and Evangelicals in particular, have been taught is actually what *the Holy Bible* teaches."

"In some cases, thankfully, it isn't! This is especially so in regard to what most Christians have been taught about eternal hell fire. Contrary to what some Fundamentalist and Evangelical bloggers have said about Bell not believing in hell, he does believe in hell, but he does not believe in literal hell fire."

"This author has a broad, expansive, redemptive view of hell which is what *the Bible* actually teaches about hell when fire is correctly understood to symbolize purification. This truth is inherent in the Greek word for fire which is 'pur,' from which, via Latin, we get our English words: pure, purity, purify, purification, purge, purgatory, etc. Biblical hell is purgatorial, so, therefore, sinners in hell can be saved. Since they have free will, which God will never violate, God will allow them to say, 'No,' to being saved as long as they want to, but, eventually, the last sinner will stop sinning and say, 'Yes,' to God's never-withdrawn offer of salvation and be saved, because LOVE WINS!"

"The Apostle Paul, in the 'love chapter,' I Cor. 13, says, about God's divine love—Greek 'agape'—'love never fails' ["N" in acrostic "Insanity"] and "love is the greatest"; how, then, can God's love not win? Bell wisely points out that the gates to the New Jerusalem are never shut, so purified sinners can return to their heavenly home where they will be reconciled and restored to God."

"Many Christians say that Jesus said more about hell than He did about heaven. Bell exposed this statement for the lie which it is, since Jesus said far more about heaven than hell. Bell also listed each occurrence in which Jesus used the word "hell," and there are only a few."

"Bell also addressed the few passages of scripture in which Jesus talked about judgment and the after life in which He did not use the word 'hell.' A prime example is Matthew 25:46 in which Jesus said that the sheep (the righteous) will be separated from the goats (the unrighteous). 'The goats are sent, in the Greek language, to an aion [actually the Greek adjective 'aionios' transliterated, 'aeonian'] of kolazo. Aion, we know, has several meanings. One is 'age' or 'period of time;' another refers to intensity of experience. The word kolazo is a term from horticulture. It refers to the pruning and trimming of the branches of a plant so it can flourish."

"An aion of kolazo. depending on how these words are translated, probably mean a period of pruning... or an intense experience of correction. It is not God's will that any perish but all come to repentance (II Pet. 3:9). Will God ever get what God wants? The answer: Job said to God, 'I know that you can do all things; no purpose of yours can be thwarted'" (42:2 RSV and NIV). **Since no plan of God can be thwarted, that includes God's plan of salvation ["T" in the acrostic "Insanity"].**

If God's saving grace is forever resisted, God's plan of salvation will be thwarted. The term "irresistible grace" does not mean saving grace cannot be resisted at all; it can be resisted indefinitely. Theoretically, it can be resisted forever, since God will not violate sinners' free will. Ultimately, saving grace will prove to be irresistible as evidenced by every created being worshiping God forever and ever (Rev. 5:13)! **This, logically, is irrefutable proof God's love is inescapable.**

God Wins

Mark Galli, the Senior Editor of *Christianity Today*, in 2011, wrote a rapid response to Bell's book, on the *New York Time's* list of best-selling books, *Love Wins: A Book About Heaven, Hell, and the Fate of Every Person Who Has*

Ever Lived. The title of Galli's book is, *God Wins: Heaven, Hell, and Why the Good News Is Better than Love Wins.*[5] [Galli said that his book was not just about Bell's book, but of 93 endnotes, 62 were to *Love Wins.*] Galli's chief complaint is that Bell's book is "incoherent." I found *Love Wins* to be perfectly coherent except for Bell's conclusion that some sinners in hell may forever say, "No," to God's saving grace and, due to their stubborn refusal to repent, remain in hell forever. On the other hand, I found Galli's book to be a paragon of incoherencies. It would take a whole book to refute all of them, but I will deal with three: title/subtitle, Galli's "fairness" objection, and an omission. *God Wins* is an excellent example of the insanity in fear-based Christianity, particularly the currently hot [pun intended] topic of hell.

First, the most glaring example of incoherence is the inherent contradiction between the title and subtitle of *God Wins* which is oxymoronic! The only thing which could be better about God *Wins* than *Love Wins* is that God would actually win. In Love *Wins*, God is loving enough to win and might finally win, but there is no assurance of it. In *God Wins*, God is a big loser in that God is either unable or unwilling to save all humanity. In Galli's Calvinistic tradition, it appears that it is a case of God being unwilling to "elect" every one for salvation, since all of the "elect" will be saved.

He appears to be a student of Jonathan Edwards (1703-1758), the Calvinist who preached the infamous spiritually insane sermon, "Sinners in the Hands of an Angry God." Edwards likened sinners to a spider on a string being held over hell by God who may well let go letting sinners plummet to their eternal doom in the fiery abyss! Galli quoted Edwards five times. Apparently, Galli has never felt like the spider on the string. For those of us who have, it is truly a horrifying experience!

The second glaring case of incoherence in *God Wins* is Galli's argument that it would be unfair for every one to be saved even though sinners, through the purging fire of hell, would be saved after ages of reaping what they had sown in life. He cited what would be two examples of such unfairness—Hitler and Osama Bin Laden. But he destroyed his fairness argument by stating that we do not know what God might do. Galli, said that God might allow Hitler and Bin Laden to repent and be saved after death but before the Final Judgment![6] He stated, "We might hope this is true...." He also suggested that Bin Laden might have gotten a "last-second chance to repent, as did the thief on the cross."[7]

If either last-second salvation or immediately after death is true, for these diabolical men, that would be the par excellence example of unfairness. Not only would Hitler and Bin Laden be saved, but God would prove Himself to be a fool! *The Bible* says that God is no fool; you reap what you sow (Gal. 6:7). But Hitler and Bin Laden would not reap what they sowed in life. If Galli is right, God will have not only saved them but also granted them a crop failure! This is spiritual insanity! It is obvious that Galli has no problem with God saving the worst of the worst of humanity—only with God saving every one. Galli's problem is not with Bell but with Jesus who said that were He crucified, He would draw all people to Himself (John 12:32).

The glaring omission in *God Wins* is any reference to Jesus' mixed metaphor in stating the purpose of hell, "For every one will be salted with fire" (Mark 9:49 KJV). The best translation of this symbolic language is in *The Good News Bible: Today's English Version*. It says, "Everyone will be purified by fire." Every one in hell purified by fire is our loving Lord's definitive statement on the purpose of hell!

After reading *God Wins*, I called the author at *Christianity Today*. He was not in, so I left a voice message. Galli graciously returned my call the same day, and we had a very stimulating discussion for about half an hour. He told me that he likes discussing theology. I asked him if he had ever heard of being "salted with fire," and he said that he had not. We talked about Jesus' mixed metaphor for awhile, and he, while we were talking, downloaded the ebook of *Spiritual Terrorism*. He remarked that he was very busy and would not be able to read it for awhile. A couple of months passed, and I left another message.

He promptly responded with an email saying that he appreciated my "spirit and sharp mind" evidenced in our conversation. But he stated that he is extremely busy so he has no plans to read *Spiritual Terrorism* any time soon, and any study of universal salvation is not a priority for him. I too appreciated the conversation we had. Galli impressed me as a personable man who is intelligent and well educated. But regardless of what he or others say about the purpose of hell, I will take Jesus'—God in the flesh—word for it. I would like to have given this book a higher rating, but due to the spiritual insanity, it merits only one star.

Jesus said that the goats would go into an aeon/age of "kolasin." Bell, in *Love Wins*, correctly stated that the Greek word "kolasin" is a horticultural term meaning to prune in order to make plants grow better. R.V.G. Tasker, the General Editor of the Evangelical commentary series, *The Tyndale New Testament Commentaries*, wisely stated that the word "aeonian," has been incorrectly translated as "everlasting" punishment for the goats. He insightfully warned, **"It would certainly be difficult to 'exaggerate' the harmful effect of this unfortunate mistranslation, particularly when fire is understood in a literal rather than a metaphorical sense."**[8] Thus, Jesus taught that hell would be an aeon/age of corrective "fire," not eternal torture!

God's Infinite Mercy

Almost all Christian Churches teach and preach that God is infinitely merciful. Yet, they also preach and teach that unless people hear about salvation in Christ, respond affirmatively, and live a good Christian life they will not go to heaven. God will, come Judgment Day, judge them, condemn them, and cast them into the lake of fire and brimstone wherein they will be tormented day and night forever and ever (Rev. 20:10)!

Psalm 136 has 26 verses, and in every verse it says that God's mercy [KJV] endures forever! That would be infinite mercy! To teach that God's mercy is infinite and then preach that it will end with sinners cast into the lake of fire and brimstone/sulfur, means that God's mercy does end. Or God will be forever mercilessly torturing sinners in spite of loving them unconditionally and being infinitely merciful! This is a blatant contradiction of the Holy Scriptures and is an excellent example of spiritual insanity! Infinite mercy cannot end or God's mercy is not infinite [the second "I" in "Insanity" acrostic—infinite mercy not enduring forever]!

Separating the Sheep and the Goats

A passage of Holy Scripture which has struck fear into the hearts of many Christians is Jesus' teaching of the separation of the righteous and unrighteous people—characterized as sheep and goats—at The Final Judgment (Mt. 25:46). Jesus taught that at the end of the present aeon/age [world, KJV] the unrighteous would go away into everlasting punishment but the righteous into life eternal, according to the KJV and some modern translations.

Shepherds tending their flocks were a very common sight in the Middle East in Biblical times. Shepherds often had mixed flocks of sheep and goats. Both sheep and goats were valuable animals for their meat, milk and cheese, and wool and hair, respectively, for making clothing. Goat's milk was particularly prized in that it was rich and nourishing. Goats and sheep had different grazing patterns. Goats could go higher on a mountain where sheep could not go. Goats would eat vegetation higher off the ground, while sheep would eat lower vegetation right down to the roots. Sometimes the goats and sheep needed to be separated for milking, grazing, shearing, tending to sickness and injuries, etc.

As Jesus said, the sheep (and goats) knew their shepherd's voice and would come to him and follow him. As the goats and the sheep came to the shepherd, he would use his staff to tap the sheep on their right side, and they would go to his right side. He would tap the goats on their left side, and they would go to his left side.

Therefore, Jesus used this metaphor of sheep and goats to teach the truth about The Final Judgment. **Of utmost importance, in interpreting Jesus' teaching, is that there would have been absolutely no thought of the good shepherd or any shepherd harming the goats**, though goats tended to be aggressive while sheep were submissive—a lot like different kinds of people.

The early Christians certainly understood that Jesus was the Good Shepherd of both sheep and goats. To avoid persecution, early Christians worshiped in the Catacombs, subterranean caverns under the city of Rome. On the walls of the Catacombs, some etchings have been found which were done by the early followers of Jesus. Some are of the Good Shepherd with a lamb on his shoulders. This imagery is deeply engrained in the Christian faith.

The image of the Good Shepherd surrounded by his sheep, with a lamb on his shoulders or in his arms, has been carved into wood, engraved on utensils and rings, woven into rugs, painted on canvas, printed in books, stitched into wall hangings, and portrayed in church stained-glass windows. But the early Christians knew and believed something which, due to the false doctrine of eternal torment in hell, has been lost to almost all Christian Churches today. This is evidenced by etchings found in the Catacombs of the Good Shepherd with a kid—a young goat on his shoulders.

An exception to this all-loving image of Jesus was the writings of Quintus Tertullian (155-222) an early church father from North Africa. His writings supported the view of the Phrygian sect which taught that if Christians should deny being a Christian after having been baptized, they could never be forgiven and were forever doomed to hell. This was their judgment even though the denial was solely due to great persecution—even torture. Matthew Arnold

(1822-1888), British Professor of Poetry at Oxford University, penned the truth of CU in these inspiring words [poem is in the writings of John Wesley Hanson (1803-1901) at tentmaker.org]:

The Good Shepherd

He saves the sheep, the goats he doth not save!
So rang Tertullian's sentence on the side
of that unpitying Phrygian sect which cried,
"Him can no fount of fresh forgiveness lave,
Whose sins once washed by the baptismal wave!"
So spake the fierce Tertullian, but she sighed,
The infant Church, of love she felt the tide
Stream on her from her Lord's yet recent grave,
And then she smiled, and in the Catacombs,
With eyes suffused but heart inspired true,
On those walls subterranean, where she hid
Her head in ignominy, death and tombs,
She her Good Shepherd's hasty image drew
And on his shoulders not a lamb, a kid!

What a fantastic understanding of the breadth and depth of the all-inclusive love of our Lord Jesus Christ! Let us recover and learn what the early Christians knew and believed—that the Good Shepherd saves goats as well as sheep! Therefore, we have the greatest story ever told to share with all people of all nations! H. Ernest Nichol (1862-1928) wrote the wonderful hymn, "We've a Story to Tell to the Nations."

We've a story to tell to the nations that shall turn their hearts to the right, a story of truth and mercy, a story of peace and light... We've a song to be sung to the nations that shall lift their hearts to the Lord, a song that shall conquer evil and shatter the spear and sword...We've a message to give to the nations that the Lord who reigneth above hath sent us His Son to save us and show us, that God is love....

The fourth stanza expresses the hope that all of the world's great peoples "might" come to the truth of God. Thanks be to God, we know based on the authority of Holy Scripture that all people shall eventually come to the truth of God (John 12:32; Phil. 2:9-11; Rev. 5:13)!

Thus, let us look forward with excited anticipation to the fulfillment of the wonderful truth expressed in the refrain of this great Christian hymn! **"For the darkness shall turn to dawning, and the dawning to noon-day bright, and Christ's great kingdom shall come to earth, the kingdom of love and light."**

The Good and The Great Shepherd

Jesus is not only the Good Shepherd, He is also the Great Shepherd (Heb. 13:20) who came to save all people. The Great Shepherd is the Savior of both goats and sheep! This concept of Jesus saving all is expressed in the title of the book, *Good Goats: Healing Our Image of God,* written by Roman Catholics Dennis, Matthew, and Sheila Linn. As a hospice chaplain for over 14 years, when dying patients were fearful of dying, due to fear of eternal damnation in hell fire, I regularly shared the healing image of God in *Good Goats* with both Catholics and Protestants who thereby were able to understand the unconditional love of God and were able to die in peace.

Discussion Questions

1. What does the term "inescapable" love of God mean?

2. What is meant by the term, "irresistible grace?" Is it not resistible at all?

3. Why/how can "irresistible grace" be resisted?

4. Theoretically, how could "irresistible grace" be resisted forever?

5. Can God's plan of salvation be thwarted or only delayed? Job said that no plan of God can be thwarted (42:2 RSV and NIV). Does that not include God's salvation plan?

6. Which makes more sense to you: God will out-love and out-last sinners resisting saving grace (since God's love [agape] is infinitely patient [I Cor. 13:4]) or God will give up on saving those resisting saving grace? Why?

7. Would God eventually winning the cosmic conflict between good and evil, give real meaning to infinite patience and endurance (I Cor. 13:4)? Why?

8. Since God's love [agape] is patient and never fails (I Cor. 13:4-8), how can God fail to win all?

Chapter 11
Triumph of God

The second "T" in the acrostic, CHRISTIANITY, represents "Triumph of God" over sin, death, and the Devil. Can you even imagine this terrible ending to the great drama of the redemptive story? Try to imagine relatively few Christians being in heaven and billions of non-Christians and the "wrong kind of Christians" being tortured in hell fire forever! Is it not extremely perverse to call such an horrific ending to God's plan, in Christ, to save the whole world, God winning? What would it take for God to win in a common-sense understanding of the word "win"?

In many situations in life, it is a case of I win, you lose. Or, in other situations, it is a matter of you win, I lose. The ideal situation, in interpersonal relations, is a win/win. There are, unfortunately, situations where two people are so stubborn that they destroy each other in trying to win at all cost, so they end up with an outcome of lose/lose—a catastrophic ending! There is an old proverb—before you seek revenge, first dig two graves—one for your enemy and another one for yourself!

Virtually everyone loves a story with a happy ending. When God is able to bring His perfect plan of salvation to a perfect ending by destroying His enemies by making them His friends and worshipers, that will truly be a win/win—the ultimate-happy ending to the great drama of redemptive history! The petition in "The Lord's Prayer" Christians have earnestly prayed throughout the centuries will have been answered, "Thy Kingdom come, Thy will be done on earth as it is in heaven."

Sharing the Good News

In 2009, I had the opportunity and pleasure of talking by phone with Dr. Ben Campbell Johnson, who had retired after teaching for more than three decades at Columbia Theological Seminary, in

Atlanta, Georgia. His ecumenical book, *Beyond 9/11: Christians and Muslims Together*,[1] had been published that year, and my book, *Spiritual Terrorism*, had been published in 2008. As authors and Presbyterians, we had some things in common. Both of us were and are interested in doing what we can to help bring about better relations with our brothers and sisters in the Islamic faith.

Since he was active in dialoguing with the Islamic community, I asked him if he believed in universal salvation, a perspective which I had found extremely helpful in sharing my Christian faith with Muslims in my many years as a hospice chaplain, ministering to dying patients in general as well as Muslims in particular. He acknowledged that this theological perspective would indeed be helpful, and he would like to believe in universal salvation. He also said that there are some verses in *the Bible* which appear to teach universalism, but there are other verses that seem to refute it.

I asked, "Have you ever heard of being 'salted with fire'?" He immediately said, "No, tell me about it." It was obvious that he was a very intelligent man with an open inquiring mind. I explained briefly about the fear in which I had grown up in a Fundamental Christian Church and how I had discovered, through long-diligent study, the words of Jesus in regard to the purpose of hell, "For every one will be salted with fire" (Mark 9:49).

We discussed the meaning of this symbolic language, in the form of a mixed metaphor, the symbolic meaning of the lake of fire and brimstone—burning sulfur, as well as Biblical verses which clearly teach universal salvation in Christ. After about an hour, Dr. Johnson said, "Well, you've convinced me!"

Certainly, few of my experiences of sharing my belief in CU have ended that positively and that quickly. He is what one would say, in regard to sharing one's faith, "low-hanging fruit."

I have talked with hundreds of Christians: laity, pastors, chaplains, seminary professors, Christian [and secular] college professors of religion, and other well-educated Christians, and virtually no one has heard of being salted with fire. The only ones who have heard of being salted with fire are the few, generally better-educated clergy, who have already come to believe in CU as a result of understanding the symbolic meaning of Jesus' words.

Almost all, as soon as they grasp where the conversation is going, assume that CU is heresy and do not want to know any more about it. They do not want to read, think, or grow in the grace and knowledge of our Lord and Savior Jesus Christ (II Peter 3:18). They have said, "That is a dangerous doctrine," since they perceive it to be a license to sin, in that they are motivated by fear.

Sharing with a Brilliant Linguist

There is a man who is truly gifted in the ability to learn languages. He teaches the Biblical languages of Hebrew, Aramaic, and Greek in the religion department of a Christian University. He also knows Arabic, German, French, Spanish, and other languages. I have known him for many years. After writing *Spiritual Terrorism*, I contacted him to see if he would like to read it and give his opinion as to its quality and validity. He said that he would but was very busy at the time, but he would get to it and give me his written evaluation. He also stated that, as a Calvinist, he would like to believe in Christian Universalism.

He volunteered to give a check for $1,000 to anyone who could convince him that *the Bible* actually teaches universal salvation [if received, I would put it toward more widely sharing the Good News of CU]. He said that he, based on God's law of proportionality, has a problem believing in eternal torment in hell. I sent a copy of my book to him to read and evaluate. Chapter 15 is, "Impossibilities for God," in which I listed the top ten reasons why the doctrine of eternal torment is impossible; # 3 is God's law of proportionality. God will not because He cannot violate His law without violating His character, something God cannot do.

A year went by, and I had not heard from him so I contacted him again. He apologized for not having gotten to it but shared that there had been a major departmental change which had taken a lot of time. He asked me to be patient and he would get to my book. He did say that it was not looking good for me in terms of my belief in Christian Universalism. He related that he had talked with every professor in the religion department of this Evangelical institution of higher education where he teaches, and 100% of the professors said that *the Bible* does teach eternal punishment.

This was my response: "It certainly does not surprise me that it does not look good for me, since you, apparently, have had conversations with only those who believe in eternal punishment. There is a Hebrew proverb which says that the first person who speaks always wins his case until the second person speaks and sets the record straight. I am glad to hear that you will listen to me speak through my book. Most people, who have read my book, have said that they 'hope it is true.' Some have believed it while others have been negative and some very hostile. You obviously have a very compassionate heart, as I have always perceived you to have, in that you told me you would like for it to be true. That shows that you do not have the malady from which many Christians and other people suffer—'elderbrotheritis'" [reference to Prodigal Son's elder brother's hostile reaction to his homecoming].

"I was and am in awe of your knowledge of the Biblical languages: Greek, Hebrew, Aramaic, as well as Arabic, and several other languages. I really appreciate your enthusiasm for learning languages. I remember hearing you say that your idea of heaven would be to continue to learn languages. Though I was reared in Arminianism—salvation by works, the insecurity of the believer, and eternal damnation in literal hell fire—I appreciate your frame of reference of the Calvinistic perspective."

"While I could not accept the limited nature of the atonement, Calvinism, as I said in my book [except for the fate of the unelect], is a beautiful theological system in which God leaves nothing to chance. It is so mentally, emotionally, and spiritually satisfying to know that the blessed Holy Trinity acts in perfect concert to bring to perfect fruition God's perfect plan of salvation. It was through you sharing with me your belief in Calvinism, that I came to be a 'Six-Point Calvinist' and later a 'Christian Universalist'" (both the same meaning—see chapter 6).

"I still vividly recall your explanation of the apparent contradiction of God's sovereignty and mankind's free will. You stated that like two ropes of a swing which go up through two holes in the ceiling, meet, and are tied together over a joist above the ceiling, so (somehow, of which we cannot know in this life) God's sovereignty and mankind's free will meet and are harmonized. That is one of the best analogies I have ever heard to explain, as you said, 'the incomprehensible.'"

"That said, however, I would contend that God's sovereignty and mankind's free will meet below and are harmonized in the salt of fire and burning sulfur, so we can know, in this life, how they are harmonized with Biblical certainty! I would like to know what you think of my addition of the 'S' to the Calvinistic TULIP. Until we talked, you, like virtually all clergy, seminary professors, and university professors of religion, with whom I have talked, had not heard of Jesus' mixed metaphor, 'salted with fire.'"

Another year passed before I heard from this brilliant language and theology professor. A few months ago he emailed me to thank me for what he called my "near-infinite patience." He reassured me that he will get around to reading *Spiritual Terrorism* and giving me his opinion in writing. I would love to have been able to include his reaction in this book, but I am still patiently waiting for his professional response.

I would be very gratified to receive the check for $1,000, but it would be far more gratifying to learn that I have been instrumental in helping this believer in Calvinism to make a slight modification [as shown in chapter 6] in his theology and come to the truth of CU.   It would be great to contemplate all the good this professor could do in teaching students about CU so they can, in turn, help change the world as Christ's ambassadors of peace.

A Convinced Universalist

William Barclay (1907-1978) was Professor of Divinity and Biblical Criticism at Glasgow University and the author of many Biblical commentaries and books, including a translation of *the New Testament, The Barclay New Testament*. Barclay was so widely respected as a Biblical scholar that some who probably did not know he was an avowed believer in CU, quoted him.

He wrote this article which I found on the Internet after my book was published. The title of Barclay's article was, "I Am a Convinced Universalist." He referenced his agreement with two of the great early church fathers, Origen (185-254) and Gregory of Nyssa (335-395) who believed in CU, and then stated, "But I want to set down not the arguments of others but the thoughts which have persuaded me personally of universal salvation."

Barclay then listed four logical arguments for Jesus eventually saving all people without exception. In the interest of keeping this book short and to the point, I have quoted only his fourth proposition. As a father who would do anything possible, including laying down my life for my children, I believe his argument for universal salvation, based on the Fatherhood of God, to be powerfully compelling and logically irrefutable.

> Fourth, I believe implicitly in the ultimate and complete triumph of God, the time when all things will be subject to him, and when God will be everything to everyone (1 Cor. 15:24-28). For me this has certain consequences. If one man remains outside the love of God at the end of time, it means that that one man has defeated the love of God, and that is impossible. **Further, there is only one way in which we can think of the triumph of God [that makes perfect sense].** If God was no more than a King or Judge, then it would be possible to speak of his triumph, if his enemies were agonizing in hell or were totally and completely obliterated and wiped out. But God is not only

King and Judge, God is *Father*—he is indeed Father more than anything else. **No father could be happy while there were members of his family forever in agony. No father would count it a triumph to obliterate the disobedient members of his family. <u>The only triumph a father can know is to have all his family back home. The only victory love can enjoy is the day when its offer of love is answered by the return of love. THE ONLY POSSIBLE FINAL TRIUMPH IS A UNIVERSE LOVED BY GOD AND IN LOVE WITH GOD</u>**[2] (bold, caps, brackets, and underlining mine).

How can anyone logically refute this argument that even one person being outside the love of God at the end of time will have defeated the love of God? That is, obviously, impossible, because God's love never fails (I Cor. 13:8)! [Remember the second "N" in the acrostic, "INSANITY?"] Part of the insanity in Christianity is God's never-failing love failing, *if the doctrine of eternal torture is true*. Thank God, it isn't true! It is as phony as a four-dollar bill!

Fallen Angels Can't be Saved, or Can They?

Virtually every Christian has heard and believes that the fallen angels cannot be saved. But I would say that if only one fallen angel should be outside the love of God, that means one created being has defeated the love of God, and that also is impossible!

I have always heard Christians say that fallen angels cannot be saved. Such believers usually cite Hebrews 2:16 which, depending on the translation, says that Jesus does not help angels [meaning fallen ones; holy angels need no redemption]. But I believe the KJV translators got it right on this verse which says, "For verily, he [Jesus] took not on him the nature of angels; but he took on him the seed of Abraham." It is self-evident, in the incarnation, Jesus took on human nature, not the nature of angels. Jesus, obviously, believed that fallen angels can and will be saved! He made a clear

179

statement, which should leave no doubt, but it is good example where starting with a false assumption leads to a false conclusion.

In his book, *Erasing Hell*, the author, Francis Chan, wrote in opposition to Rob Bell's book, *Love Wins*. As already explained, Bell put forth the proposition that God might save the whole human race. My only disagreement with Bell is that he only said God may save every one, rather than definitely stating that God shall save the whole world.

The Bible claims God loves the world and Christ, as the Savior of the world, shall save the world (John 1:29; 3:16; 4:42; Phil. 2:9-11). Chan believes *the Bible* clearly teaches that not every one will be saved, and fallen angels have no chance of being saved.[3] Why?

First, I want to give credit to Rev. Chan. In carefully reading *Erasing Hell*, I was impressed that Chan had done a lot of research, had done serious thinking about difficult theological issues, and had written with conviction but also compassion. He self disclosed that he would like for universal salvation to be true, but said, of course, wishing so does not make it true. He expressed openness to the prospect that hell may be for annihilation of sinful people so, at least, they will not be tormented forever. What compassionate person would not at least hope for that, since annihilation would be immeasurably more humane than God torturing sinners forever?[4]

Chan also stated that the fire of hell is metaphorical, not literal. He even addressed the issue of mixed metaphors such as fire and darkness. Chan wisely counseled that where two symbols are mutually exclusive—fire producing light and darkness being the absence of light—they should be taken as just that—"metaphors." He cited the opinions of several leading Evangelicals, including Dr. Billy Graham, in support of this common-sense understanding. So what disagreement do I have with Chan on hell?[5]

He said that the Greek word "aeonian" must mean eternal, everlasting, or forever. He referenced Matthew 25:46 to bolster his position. In this verse Jesus said the righteous and the unrighteous, at The Final Judgment, will be separated. The unrighteous will go away into "aeonian" punishment and the righteous into life "aeonian." Moulton and Milligan, two widely renowned authorities on Greek, in their massive work, *The Vocabulary of the Greek Testament*, clearly expressed the meaning of the word "aeonian."[6]

They stated that regardless of the meanings theologians have vested in the word, it means that of which "the horizon is not in view, whether it is at an infinite distance or no longer than the span of a Caesar's life."[7] Thus, it can mean eternal or a short period of time. They also said that the Greek word translated as punishment is a term from horticulture meaning to prune in order to make plants grow better. It would, therefore, not make sense to say that spiritual pruning of sinners in hell will go on forever.

But Chan concluded that hell is forever, so no one can be saved, because there is no longer an opportunity to be saved. Very significantly, he based his conclusion on Mt. 25:41 where Jesus, "The King," tells the unrighteous to depart into the "aeonian" fire prepared for the Devil and his angels. Chan's reasoning is that since fallen angels can't be saved and human sinners are in the same fire, then no one in hell can be saved. If Chan's assumption that fallen angels can't be saved were true, then he would be correct to conclude human sinners in hell cannot be saved. But I looked at the same two verses, Mt. 25:41, 46, over a quarter of a century ago and drew the opposite conclusion. My rationale?

I stated in Spiritual Terrorism that those in hell, people and angels, will have a common fate. If the purpose of hell is penal only, they will be tormented forever. If it is for annihilation, they will cease to exist. But if hell is for the purpose of purification, both humans and fallen angels will be purified, reconciled, and restored to God.

As I explained in the chapter on "Symbolism of Fire," Jesus' mixed metaphor, "salted with fire," in regard to sinners in hell, means exactly what He said. "For everyone will be purified by fire," which is how *The Good News Bible: Today's English Version*

181

translated this symbolic language (Mark 9:49). Based on Jesus' authority that all humans in hell will be purified by fire, I came to the only possible **logical** conclusion in regard to fallen angels.

Connecting the dots or verses, since humans and fallen angels will be in the same fire, both will eventually be saved. Christ will draw all to Himself (John 12:32), all will live in Christ (I Cor. 15:22), and God will become all in all (I Cor. 15:28). It is only a question of when, not if, every knee bows and every tongue confesses Jesus Christ as Lord to the glory of God (Phil. 2:9-11). Ditto that for when every created being in the universe begins worshiping God and the Lamb eternally (Rev. 5:13)! All those "under the earth," in both Phil. 2:9-11 and Rev. 5:13, are human sinners and fallen angels having been purified by the same fire.

Restoring the Church and the World

After grasping the glorious truth of CU, what needs to be done to restore the Christian Church to what Jesus taught and restore the world by bringing it into harmony with God and all created beings? In the chapter, "The Next Big Shift," of *The Next Generation: The Good News About The End Of Christian America*,[8] Gable Lyons expressed very insightful, profoundly enlightening, intensely practical, and potentially transformative observations and recommendations for the future restoration of the Christian Church. Lyons used the words "restore," "restoration," "restorative," or "restoring" repeatedly in this chapter.

The subject of CU is not even mentioned in this book, but concepts of restoration, which would logically lead to belief in CU, are prominent. When quoting pertinent passages, I have capitalized the word "restore" and its various forms for emphasis.

Lyons wisely stated that the first thing Christians must do is rediscover the Gospel—"to **relearn** and fall in love again with that historic, beautiful, redemptive, faithful, demanding, reconciling, all-powerful, RESTORATIVE, atoning, grace-abounding, soul-quenching, spiritually fulfilling good news of God's love. Following Jesus in the twenty-first century demands that his disciples **relearn** the full meaning of the Gospel story, recovering the culminating theme of RESTORATION that runs throughout the whole of Scripture (bold mine). This begins by seeing the Gospel as the central resolution to humanity's age-old...conflict."

"But this story isn't static; it dynamically continues to unfold today, displaying God's original goodness and ultimate intention for all his creation. The good news for humankind is that we are all made in God's image, given a path through Jesus to be reconciled from our sin, and purposed to partner with him to renew and RESTORE the creation to its fullest potential."[9]

FANTASTIC! "RESTORE the creation to its FULLEST POTENTIAL," that would be 100 percent, wouldn't it? That would be UNIVERSAL RESTORATION (Acts 3:21 NRSV). Lyons insightfully declared, "The RESTORATIVE work of Jesus as displayed through the Gospel is the main thing...."[10]

Furthermore, Lyons explained, "...the mind-set of RESTORATION we've been discussing may appear to contrast with the conventional Christian outlook that emphasizes personal salvation and discipleship. But the opposite is true...The fact is where Christians RESTORE, people get saved." Christianity grew by some 40 percent in each decade during the first three centuries after Christ...these Christians were involved in the fabric of society, constantly RESTORING and demonstrating a better way to live...Early followers of Jesus showed up and exemplified what RESTORATION living looked like." "If this Gospel—the Gospel of Jesus Christ—is going to reengage Western culture in a new way, it starts with us. And it will happen when we commit to demonstrating his RESTORATIVE power everywhere we show up and to everyone we encounter...." "The Gospel of RESTORATION extends over all of God's creation.... "[11]

A Treasure Trove of Vital Information

The Next Christians and *unChristian* are both terrific books! They are, indeed, a treasure trove of information based on scientific polling, which if heeded, would soon transform the Christian Church in America and Christianity worldwide. I cannot recommend these books more strongly! They should be read by all Christians individually, studied in adult and youth Sunday school classes, and home Bible studies. Combined, these books comprise almost 500 pages of charts, graphs, and other data from research on what Americans think of Christians and the Christian Church.

The Apostle Paul said that Christians are open letters read by all people (II Cor. 3:1-3). The American public is reading what they see in the lives of Christians, and they do not like what they are reading in their attitudes and behavior. But there is great potential for healthy change. Lyons is right on in his assessment of the opportunity for transformation of Christians and the church. "When Christians recover the effect of the Gospel in their own lives to shift their inclinations from judgment to grace, hypocrisy to authenticity, and rejection to acceptance, then outsiders will give them another chance."[12]

But change will not happen as long as Christians hold onto the false and divisive doctrine of eternal torture in hell fire as well as their eschatology—end-of-the-world fatalism—the Mark of the Beast, the Rapture of the Church, the Great Tribulation, and the world-ending fiery holocaust. In *Spiritual Terrorism*, I addressed the issue of the Mark of the Beast in some detail. The key factor is that this is not the mark of "a man" (Rev. 13:18) as the KJV and other versions have translated it. *The New International Version* (NIV) [the best-selling modern translation] correctly translated the Greek as "man's number," which makes a significant difference.

The Rapture of the Church may sound positive if you are the "right kind of Christian," but the "wrong kind of Christians" and all non-Christians will be left here on earth to endure the horror of The Great Tribulation at the hands of the merciless anti-Christ. An example of this theological perspective, in regard to The Rapture, is this posting on Facebook. "IN CASE OF RAPTURE ALL BELIEVERS ON FACEBOOK WILL BE GONE." So all "unbelievers" will be left according to the fatalistic belief that, through persecution and war, a third of the human race [over two billion people] will be killed (Rev. 9) before Christ returns for His Second Advent and sets up His millennial reign of peace. That is the pre-millennial view of Christ's Second Advent. But as I pointed out in *Spiritual Terrorism*, Christ is probably not going to bail out the "born-again" Christians who, with their fatalistic end-of-the-world literalism, may have helped create a self-fulfilling prophecy.

The human race can learn to live in peace, without having a fiery holocaust and Christ coming to impose peace. Learning to live in peace will bring Christ's kingdom of love and light to our world of hatred and spiritual darkness. This is the post-millennial view of Christ's Second Advent which will restore the world.

A Glorious Future for the Church and the World

This is Lyons' RESTORATIVE view of the future: "The next Christians are breathing new life into a movement that, in some ways, was sputtering at the close of the last century. Ready for tomorrow's challenges, they turn toward the twenty-first-century horizon with grace in their hands and the Gospel as their calling. They are RESTORING confidence in their faith and turning 'Christian' into a label worthy of the one who has called them to RESTORE."[13] I am in 100 percent agreement! This attitudinal and behavioral change will truly inspire people to be like our loving Lord and our heavenly Father, resulting in universal salvation, universal peace, and universal restoration!

As I have reported, Biblical literalists have a fatalistic view of the future of the world ending in a fiery holocaust. There have been over the centuries hundreds of prophecies about the end of the world. Harold Camping twice predicted the end of the world in 2011. And the Mayan Calendar predicts it for December 21, 2012. Don't worry, I have a perfect predictive record. The world will last as long as it takes for people to learn to live in peace. That will not happen by December 21, 2012, so the world will not end then.

But this wonderful truth is not just Good News that every created being will be saved some glorious day; it has implications for world peace while humans are living on planet earth. There are various prophecies in *the Old Testament (The Torah)* which foretell peace on earth. But Evangelical Christians, due to a fatalistic view of eschatology—end-of-the-world theology—relegate all prophecies of peace on earth to the Millennial Reign of Christ. They believe that mankind is too sinful to ever make peace on earth, and the world will experience a fiery holocaust which will signal the Second Coming of Christ. Thus, world peace is only possible when Christ comes for His Second Advent and imposes peace. This is the pre-millennial view of Christ's Second Coming.

Other Christians believe that we can achieve peace on earth without experiencing a world-ending holocaust, and the time will come when our weapons of war are recycled into implements of agriculture [swords into plowshares and spears into pruning hooks] and young people will learn and fight wars no more (Isaiah 2:4). This is called the amillennial view [meaning no millennium] which means that humans will learn to live in peace without Christ returning at all. The post-millennial view means that Christ will return after mankind has learned to live in peace.

Thus, world peace is possible, but it must begin with each believer doing all one can to be a peaceful person and to live in peace with all of our brothers and sisters in the human family. In 1955 the authors of, "Let There Be Peace On Earth" captured this truth that there can be peace on earth without having a holocaust.

Jill Jackson Miller stated online, "And when I attempted suicide and I didn't succeed, I knew for the first time unconditional love—which God is. God is unconditional love. You are totally loved, totally accepted, just the way you are. Something difficult to explain happened to me. I had an eternal moment of truth, in which I knew I was loved, and knew I was here for a purpose."

Thus, Miller movingly speaks of her life—how she became an orphan as a young girl, her hardship of being in foster care, and her depression—all of which led to her attempted suicide at age 42. She shared that it was this time, described above, in which she became aware of the presence of a higher power in her life and how she came to write her now worldwide-famous song. It has been translated into various languages, and is sung around the world expressing universal aspiration for peace. Jill Jackson Miller's daughter, the copyright holder, who desires anonymity, graciously gave permission to use this wonderful song.

Let There Be Peace On Earth
By Jill Jackson Miller and Sy Miller

Let there be peace on earth
And let it begin with me;
Let there be peace on earth,
The peace that was meant to be.

With God as our Creator*
We are family, *
Let us walk with each other*
In perfect harmony.

Let peace begin with me,
Let this be the moment now;
With every step I take,
Let this be my solemn vow:

To take each moment and live each moment
In peace eternally.
Let there be peace on earth
And let it begin with me.

We can have peace on earth by making a personal vow to be an instrument of peace with the mission, "Let there be peace on earth, and let it begin with me." I agree with the late Dr. Martin Luther King, Jr. that the moral arc of the universe is long, but it bends toward justice. The arc of God's perfect justice bends to universal salvation and universal peace!

Discussion Questions

1. Do you think God would be satisfied with God wins/sinners lose scenario? Why?

2. What about sinners winning/God losing scenario?

3. Do you think God could have a win/win without violating anyone's free will? How?

4. Does it make sense that Christian Universalism would help in interfaith dialog and relations? Why?

5. Are Jesus' words "salted with fire" literal or worse? Does this mixed metaphor symbolize purification? Why?

6. In your opinion, what will constitute God's final triumph?

7. Have you heard and believe fallen angels can't be saved? Does it make sense that, since sinners in hell and fallen angels are in the same fire both will be saved?

8. Dualism means that good and evil will forever be in conflict. Eternal "damnationists" claim that this is bad theology. Would not eternal evil even in hell be dualistic forever blighting God's Kingdom of love and light?

9. St. Gregory of Nyssa (335-395) said when God is all in all [KJV]—everything to every one [RSV] (1 Cor. 15:28) evil will be extinct, since sin will have no place to reside. Do you agree or disagree? Why?

Chapter 12
You Shall Know the Truth that Frees

The "Y" in the acrostic, "CHRISTIANITY," represents, "You Shall Know the Truth that Frees" from fear. Jesus said, "You shall know the truth, and the truth shall make you free" (John 8:32). Questions of the utmost importance are: what is the truth that frees from fear, and how can you find it? You can find it in *The Holy Bible,* but with so many churches interpreting *the Bible* in so many different ways, how can a person ever know for sure what is true and what isn't? The answer is to read, study, think for oneself, and grow in the grace and knowledge of Christ (II Peter 3:18).

Sadly, the last place one is likely to find the truth that frees from fear is in most Christian Churches. I do not mean to be unkind, and I do not want to be divisive. Yes, there are various spiritual truths, but I am referring specifically to the truth of Christian Universalism (CU). Today, there are very few Christian Churches teaching this glorious truth. You may hear about CU but probably not in the vast majority of churches unless you hear it being preached about as an example of heretical Christian doctrine.

I have always wanted to know the truth. As they say in court proceedings, "The truth, the whole truth, and nothing but the truth." The truth may be unpleasant, even painful, but I can handle the truth. Lies only make matters worse.

Jesus Stands at the Door and Knocks

A very popular verse in *the Bible* that is often used in inviting unsaved sinners to confess their sins and personally accept Jesus as their Lord and Savior contains Jesus' words, "Behold, I stand at the door, and knock: if any man hear my voice, and open the door, I will come in to him..." (Rev. 3:20). Christians, who use this verse in this way, are taking it out of its Biblical context. What is the context? Jesus is actually standing outside the door of the church

189

asking to be welcomed in. What? What a contrast! Jesus is having to ask to be welcomed into the church He founded and of which He is proclaimed to be the Head. There is even a popular painting of Jesus standing outside this door without a handle indicating that the would-be believer must open the door from the inside to let Jesus in. What is wrong with this picture? The Revelation was written to the Christian churches, not to unbelievers. Has the Christian Church lost the message Jesus taught and gone so far off track that Jesus has to ask for permission to come into His own church?

What Message Did Jesus Teach?

Just *as surely as the grass is green, the sky is blue, God is in heaven, and Christ is Lord, Jesus taught Messianic/Christian [Hebrew: Messiah equals Greek: Christ] Universalism (CU)!* The apostles preached it, and the early church believed it for well over 500 years—long [more than 200 years] after the Christian Church had become the state church of the Roman Empire. As I have explained in this book and covered more extensively in *Spiritual Terrorism*, Origen, the church's first systematic theologian, believed in and taught CU. He was born in 185 and died in 254 at the age of 69 in full communion [good standing] with the Christian Church to which he had devoted his godly life and work. Origen, his writings, and his memory were condemned by the Fifth General Council of the church in the year 553. Thus, Origen had been dead for 299 years before he was unjustly condemned!

Why was Origen condemned posthumously? Today, there is some dispute about this great miscarriage of justice, but the real reason seems to have been for believing in and teaching CU although some other reasons were given, perhaps as a smoke screen. The Catholic authors of *Good Goats: Healing Our Image of God*[1] reported that Origen was condemned for reasons other than universalism, and that it is now okay to teach universalism in the Roman Catholic Church. I am certainly glad to hear that, but the perception seems to have been that the condemnation—Origen, his writings, and his memory—included universalism.

190

In fact, in *The Teaching of Christ, A Catholic Catechism For Adults,* the editors stated, "Some early theologians, notably Origen in the third century, took the position that all sinners, including Satan, will eventually be brought to salvation. This and similar views, however, the Church has **always** (bold mine) decisively rejected, as incompatible with revealed truth, and the Church has solemnly confirmed the doctrine that punishment in hell is eternal." In a footnote they also reported, "The doctrine of eternity of hell was solemnly taught by the Fourth Lateran Council, November 1215, The Catholic Faith (DS 801)."[2] Eternal hell is reaffirmed [but more nuanced] in the latest *Catechism of the Catholic Church* (1992), translated into English in 1994.[3]

If Christian Universalism was not condemned with Origen, there has been a terrible misunderstanding for about 1,500 years! The Pope needs to restore spiritual sanity by making a definite unambiguous statement validating CU for the Catholic Church and to the world! While he is at it, the Pope also needs to clear and restore Origen's good name and declare him to be a saint in the Catholic Church. Pope Benedict XVI is not a good candidate for doing this, because he did his doctoral dissertation on the life of Saint Augustine (354-430), whom the Pope has held up to Catholic youth as a great example of Christian faith.

To be fair to Augustine, I must add that he was not a harsh man. He seemed fair to his theological opponents who believed in CU in that he acknowledged there were "very many" of them, and he called them "tender hearts," not "unorthodox" or "heretics." [For more info on early church fathers, Google: De Civ. Dei, lib. 21, c. 17 or Encheirid. Ad Laurent, c. 29.] It is significant to note that Augustine was born in 354 which was 100 years after the death of Origen. Augustine died at the age of 76, in 430. <u>It would be another 123 years before Origen's condemnation.</u>

Augustine fathered a child out of wedlock and would not marry his child's mother. He taught that unbaptized infants will be forever banished from God's presence or, infinitely worse, be punished forever because they had the misfortune to be born, as all are, with original sin! No person has had a more profoundly negative influence on Christianity in the West (Western Europe and North and South America) than Augustine. He deserves a lot of blame for the insanity in Christianity—eternal torture in hell.

Augustine had great power of persuasion. By this power and the corrupting influence of power-hungry church officials [or those too cowardly to stand against evil] and control-freak Roman Emperors, the truth of CU was later changed to salvation for a few and eternal damnation for the vast majority of humanity. This was for the purpose of controlling the masses of uneducated citizens through fear of the government and eternal torment in hell fire. The church has been living with this sad legacy for about 1,500 years with Christians in the West believing that the lie of eternal torture is the truth, and the truth of CU is a lie! Riley and William have done a good job of researching the life of Augustine in their book, *"Is God Fair? What about Gandhi?*[4]

The Vatican probably has the most extensive library on religious documents in the world, and the truth of CU, without a doubt, is there in the archives. Lay people do not need access to the Vatican Library; they can find a wealth of information on Christian Universalism on the Internet. I am confident there will be a Pope, eventually, with the desire for truth that frees (John 8:32). It would be a courageous act if the Pope would do the right thing in regard to correcting the great wrong done to Origen. This would validate CU for the Catholic Church and to the world. This will be a significant development on the exceedingly long road to Christian reconciliation and world peace!

It appeared that Pope John Paul II either believed in CU or was very close. He was definitely making progress in interfaith dialogue, of which the perspective of universal salvation would be of immense benefit. But under Pope Benedict XVI the church seems to have regressed. **Claiming that you are the head of the only true religion, having the mantle of infallibility with a monopoly on salvation, and then seeking better relations with the members of other religions is a nonstarter.**

For readers who would like to have more information on the history of the Christian Church in regard to CU, I recommend Bob Evely's book of only 173 pages, *At the End of the Ages: the Abolition of Hell.*[5] This author has done a good job of researching and reporting on early church fathers who believed in CU as well as other Christian believers in CU throughout the centuries.

There is a growing body of literature on CU in new books in print, ebooks, Internet websites and blogs, and other sources. Sadly, the least likely place seekers of the truth of CU are likely to find it is in Christian Churches! And the more conservative they are, the more likely they will be resistive and even hostile to the Good News of CU. I truly wish this were not the case, but my experiences, observations, and reading of history say it is.

I have heard pastors who preach on the radio make various statements which, if followed to their logical conclusion, would lead people to the truth of CU. This is also true of the writings of published works of Christian authors. When this has happened, I have tried to get contact information and call them to talk by phone or to get an appointment to discuss their statements with them in person. The following are Christian pastors, writers, and other Christians with whom I have talked. They represent typical officials in Christian Churches early in the 21st Century.

Trusting God for too Much Rather than too Little

I heard the pastor of a large Evangelical Church preaching on the radio several months ago that he does not want to be guilty of anything, but if he is guilty of something, he wants to be guilty of trusting God for too much rather than too little. I immediately thought, wow, what a great statement, ditto that for me! This was said in the context of the beginning of a building program to better minister to the church members and to reach out and win more lost souls to Christ before it is eternally too late.

The next day I called the church and asked if it would be possible to speak with the senior pastor. I was told that he was out of his office, but I could leave a message. I told the receptionist that I had heard him make a wonderful statement on the radio the day before, and I would like to get an appointment to talk with him about it. She replied that he likes to have feedback from radio listeners, so he would probably be glad to talk with me. She called back a couple of days later and scheduled a time, about a month later, for me to have a meeting with the pastor.

Meeting in his office, he seemed like a very nice man who sincerely wanted to share the Gospel with as many people as possible. We talked about our common backgrounds for about half an hour. Both of us had grown up in Fundamentalism, and both of us had traveled a long way along the road of life toward finding much more of God's love and grace than we heard about while growing up. We then talked for about another half hour about his statement of trusting God for too much, not too little.

I asked him if this matter of trusting God for too much had greater ramifications than just a building program such as bodily healing, salvation of souls, social justice, world peace, etc. He replied that it could, but you run into the problem of human free will in making other applications. I said it appears that free will is always a potential problem including a building program, since people could use their free will to choose not to give of their time, talents, and money. He then seemed a bit uneasy and asked me where the conversation was going. I replied that I see a much broader application of his terrific statement about not trusting God for too little.

I then asked him if he had ever heard of being "salted with fire," and he said that he had not. I next asked him if he knew the definition of brimstone, as in "the lake of fire and brimstone," in The Revelation." He again said, "No." Lastly, I told him that as a child, teenager, and young adult, I had been terrified of being judged and condemned by God at the end of life or the end of the world. Thus, I would be thrown into the lake of fire and brimstone wherein I would be tormented day and night forever and ever! He, too, had been afraid of eternal hell fire.

194

I shared with him that I am a seminary graduate and had been a pastor for 15 years before I had thought to look up the word "brimstone" to see exactly what it meant. I told him that brimstone means "sulfur" and asked him if he knew what sulfur was widely known for in the ancient world, long before and after *the Bible* was written. He confessed that he did not know.

When I explained to him the various beneficial uses of sulfur, as explained in the chapter on "Symbolism of Fire" in this book, he quickly "connected the dots" between sinners being "salted with fire" and being healed or disinfected of their sins in "the lake of burning sulfur." He stated that he believes that sinners have no chance to be saved after death and that the church has always believed in the doctrine of eternal punishment in hell. He then asked me a challenging question.

That question was, "What will you do when you face God at The Final Judgment and find you have been wrong about universal salvation?" I said, "That is a very good question." I will say, "God, I am sorry, I trusted you for too much rather than too little." I then asked him what he will say at The Final Judgment when he finds that he has been wrong concerning the doctrine of eternal damnation, "God, I am sorry, I trusted you for too little…?"

At that point, he looked at his watch and remembered he needed to make a phone call. As we shook hands, I told him that if he would like to have more information he could visit my website or read my book *Spiritual Terrorism.* He responded that he would be "willing to receive" a book from me, but he was so busy that he could give me no indication when he would be able to read it. I took that as never. I would estimate that, as the senior pastor of that large church, he is making a salary far in excess of $100,000. He is living in one of the most affluent areas in his city of residence. If he were interested in learning, he could certainly afford to buy my book. As a retired hospice chaplain, I am living on Social Security and a meager retirement income, but if he had said that he would love to learn more and would be glad to read it ASAP, I would have gladly given him a copy of my book.

After having grown out of the legalism in which he was reared, this pastor has apparently reached a theological comfort level with salvation by grace and the security of the believer. Evidently, he does not want to go beyond that level and risk losing his prestigious pastoral position, large income, benefits, and retirement. Having been there and done that, I fully understand the difficulty of taking a stand, being declared a heretic to the Christian faith and struggling to survive emotionally and financially. The easy way not to experience such hardships is to ignore the Biblical admonition to grow in the grace and knowledge of our Lord and Savior Jesus Christ (II Peter 3:18).

This Evangelical pastor is by no means alone. There are many more, probably the vast majority, just like him. This is why I contend the last place Christians are likely to be able to find the truth that frees from fear is in church. This definitely is true of Fundamental and Evangelical Churches. Eternal punishment is the official position of the Roman Catholic Church, but the Catholic writers Dennis, Matthew, and Sheila Linn, have the Catholic seal of approval to write from the perspective of CU. They stated in the introduction of their book, *Good Goats: Healing Our Image of God,* that universal salvation is an "entirely orthodox perspective."

The Gates of Hell, not the Gates of the Church

I heard the pastor of another Evangelical Church preach on Matthew 16:18. In this verse Jesus said, "...upon this rock, I will build my church, and the gates of hell shall not prevail against it." He correctly told his congregation something I had come to see a quarter of a century ago but had never heard a pastor preach this truth. He stated that Jesus did not say "the gates of the church" but, rather, "the gates of hell." After gaining this insight, I have asked many Christians in regard to this teaching of Jesus, which is on the offense and defense—the church or hell? They have always said, "The church is on the defense, and hell is on the offense."

Thus, the church has a "fortress mentality." Christians' theme song about "holding the fort" against the attacks of Satan and his demons, could well be Luther's hymn. "A Mighty Fortress Is Our God a bulwark never failing; our helper He amid the flood of mortal ills prevailing. For still our ancient foe [Satan] doth seek to work us woe; his craft and power are great, and armed with cruel hate, on earth is not his equal." Members are thus praying, hoping, and "keeping their fingers crossed" that Christ will come for His Second Advent in the nick of time to save the church from being overrun and destroyed by the hordes of hell! When I have pointed out that it is the gates of hell being assaulted and the gates rammed down by the church thus destroying hell, they have exclaimed, "O my goodness, I never saw that before. That changes everything!" Indeed, it does and logically leads to the truth that frees from fear!

I called and got an appointment to talk with this pastor. He seemed like a very sincere man; he was friendly, and we had a cordial conservation. I commended him on his insight into the Holy Scriptures and asked him if he saw any ramifications based on his discovery of this Biblical truth. He replied that it means Satan's destruction is assured. I asked if that means Satan will be annihilated so he will cease to exist. He granted that as a possibility, but he stated that he believes in what the Christian Church has always believed which is eternal punishment in hell.

I then asked whether he had heard of being "salted with fire," and he said that he had not. I asked if he knew the meaning of the word "brimstone" as in "the lake of fire and brimstone" in The Revelation. He replied that he did not. I informed him that it means "sulfur" and asked if he had any idea of what sulfur was widely known for in Biblical times. He responded that he did not, but he quickly grasped the potential meaning for CU. He declared, "If every one is going to be saved, Christ died for nothing!" I said, "Let me see if I understand what you are saying. If Christ, without violating any sinner's free will, gets all sinners saved, He died for nothing. But if, without violating anyone's free will, He should only get, say 10% saved, He died for something." He thought for a few moments, and then replied, "Well, 100% is better than 10%, isn't it?" I said, "Yes, indeed, 90% better!"

This pastor then looked at his watch and told me that he had to go conduct a funeral. As we shook hands, I asked him if he would like to read a book, *Spiritual Terrorism*, which I had written. He said that it sounded interesting, but he did not have much time to read. He then asked how long it is. I told him that it is about 500 pages, but I have a one-page summary that I would give him, and he could decide if he wants to read the book. He said, "Give me the summary; I can handle that." I later called to follow up with him, but he was not in. I left a message on his voice mail, but I have not heard from him. I did, however, later hear him still preaching the doctrine of eternal damnation.

Not Interpreting Bible with Preconceived Notions

I heard another pastor on the radio preaching that one must not interpret *the Bible* with preconceived notions. I called and scheduled an appointment with him. He was a pastor old enough to retire but still enjoyed preaching the Gospel. He seemed like a very nice man with a gentle spirit, who sincerely wanted unsaved people to be saved before it is forever too late. He was so kind to even treat me to lunch.

I told him that he had, in my opinion, stated a truism in saying that one must not interpret *the Bible* while holding preconceived notions. But I asked, "While that should be the mindset of all who seek to interpret *the Bible*, in the final analysis, how is that possible? Since potentially, every one has some preconceived ideas due to our religious instructions or lack thereof, how can we be sure that we are interpreting *the Bible* in the right way?" He acknowledged the validity of what I was saying and said that we all need to be open to the possibility that our thinking could be faulty. Thus, insufficient information or misinformation could cause people to misinterpret *the Bible*. We were in agreement on this common-sense understanding.

Since he had preached on eternal punishment for all those who do not accept Christ before death, I asked him if he had ever heard of being "salted with fire." He said that he had not. I asked him about the definition of brimstone and the beneficial meanings of sulfur, and he knew of neither. When I explained this symbolism to him and the implications of it, he said that he had no problem with that understanding. He stated that he had never heard of this before in spite of being a senior citizen and a lifetime of pastoring an Evangelical Church. Without my asking, he said he would like to check out my website, "HealingSpiritualTerrorism.com" and read my book.

This open-minded pastor asked an excellent question no one had previously asked. "Assuming the doctrine of CU is true, and since the early churches may have had only one book of what was later to become the collection of books called, *The Holy Bible*, how could they have understood the truth of CU?" I said that all the early churches had *the Torah* [O.T.] and the oral tradition of the life, ministry, teachings, death, resurrection, and ascension of Jesus. Even if the early Christians had only one book of the N.T., there is a verse [or verses] in almost all books that teach(es) CU.

Some are: the destruction of Hell (Mt. 16:18); being "salted with fire" (Mark 9:49), the Parable of the Good Shepherd and the Prodigal Son (Luke 15); the Rich Man in Hades/hell (Luke 16); Jesus saying He would draw all people to Himself (John 12:32); heaven receiving Christ until the time of universal restoration (Acts 3:21); God is impartial (Rom. 2:11) and all living via the righteousness of [Christ] and receiving justification of life (Rom. 5:18); God's love [agape] never fails and all live in Christ and God will be all in all (I Cor. 13:8; 15:22, 28); God was in Christ reconciling the world unto Himself (II Cor. 5:19); through Abraham shall all people be blessed (Gal. 3:8); God gathering all in Christ in heaven and on earth (Eph. 1:10); universal submission and confession that Jesus is Lord (Phil. 2:9-11); Christ making peace through the blood of the cross for all in heaven and on earth (Col. 1:20); God has not appointed us to wrath but to obtain salvation by Christ (I Thess. 5:9); [God] will have all to be saved... (I Tim. 2:4); the Grace of God has appeared bringing salvation to all (Titus 2:11); God is a consuming fire [consuming sin, purifying sinners] (Heb. 12:29); God is impartial; love your neighbor as yourself and be impartial (James 2:1, 8, 9); God is patient, not wanting any to perish but all to come to repentance (II Peter 3:9); God is love [loving all people unconditionally] (I John 4:8); all creation worshiping God and the Lamb (Rev. 5:13); the Devil, the beast, and the false prophet, are thrown into "the lake of burning sulfur" [symbolizing being disinfected and healed of sin and the destruction of death and Hades/hell] (Rev. 20:10-15).

Did Jesus Really Say That?

I talked with the pastor of a large Evangelical Church, with a contemporary style of worship which attracts a lot of young people. He told me that he has a problem with the doctrine of eternal torment and does not preach much about hell. In fact, he shared that he had preached a series of sermons, "Did Jesus Really Say That?" One of these sermons was on the subject of eternal punishment. While the pastor had questioned this senseless doctrine, he stated that he had concluded Jesus really had said that about hell fire in which sinners will be tormented forever.

I asked this pastor if he had ever heard of being "salted with fire." He said that he had not. I then asked him if he knew the definition of the word "brimstone" and the uses of sulfur in Biblical times, and he confessed that he had no idea about either. I explained that "salted with fire" is a mixed metaphor which Jesus used to state the purpose of hell, and that every way sulfur was used in the ancient world had a beneficial meaning. It was not until centuries later that the Chinese discovered a way to use sulfur to make gunpowder. I informed him that I have a whole chapter of 21 pages on "Salt of Fire and Burning Sulfur," in my book, *Spiritual Terrorism*, and I asked if he would like to read it.

I would have given him a copy had he said that he would like to but could not afford it. But he simply said that he had no interest in reading it. This Evangelical pastor questioned whether Jesus had said that about eternal torment but had never even heard of Jesus' mixed metaphor. Yet, he still had no interest in reading and learning anything more about what Jesus actually said and taught on the subject of hell. I pointed out that information on my website is free, but he was not interested.

Consequently, he will go on preaching that Jesus really did teach the insanely false doctrine of eternal torture. How sad, sick, pathetic, and typical of Fundamental and Evangelical pastors and other Christian clergy! This pastor is a young man who could have an even more effective and long ministry sharing the truth which Jesus said would set people free of fear. He is choosing to instill and exacerbate rather than ameliorate the fear in which so many Christians live. This is spiritual insanity!

How to Know You're Always Right and Never Wrong

An Evangelical pastor on a radio program preached on "How to Know You're Always Right and Never Wrong." That sounds really great but does not make sense. No person can know that he or she is always right and never wrong. I called this pastor and asked about meeting with him to discuss the message he had preached on his radio ministry. He told me that he did not have time to meet with me but asked me why I was calling. I told him how terrific the title of his message was but asked him how that is possible.

He stated that *the Bible* is so clear, plain, and simple that all a person has to do is read *the Bible* and do exactly as it says, and one can be sure of always being right and never wrong. Readers, you need to understand that this pastor is in a denomination that preaches and teaches eternal torment for all people who have not accepted Christ, including all those who never even heard of Christ before they died. And, even worse, if people have accepted Christ, made a profession of faith in Christ, or confirmed their infant baptism by confessing faith in Christ and joining a church, that is not good enough to be accepted into heaven. Believers must also be baptized by immersion in order to gain admission to heaven. This requirement of adult only immersion would exclude the vast majority of Christians—almost two billion Anglicans, Eastern Orthodox, Roman Catholics, and virtually all mainline Protestant Christians! This illustrates being the "wrong kind of Christians."

I asked this pastor if he knows *the Bible* so well that he is sure he is missing nothing. He stated that he did. I asked him my three qualifying questions: "salted with fire"; the definition of "brimstone"; and "the beneficial uses of sulfur in Biblical times." He answered in the negative of any knowledge of these issues on all three counts. I then asked him how he could know he is right and never wrong when he is not even aware of parts of *the Bible*. He was stumped but asked how he could learn more about this. I told him he could read my book or check out a lot of free info on my website: HealingSpiritualTerrorism.com.

He said that he may check it out but expressed no commitment to do so, and I have heard nothing from him. I later heard him again preaching that people will be condemned to hell fire forever for not accepting Christ, or, even if they have accepted Christ, for not being baptized by immersion.

Did Jesus Say More about Hell than about Heaven?

A preacher on the radio, preaching on eternal damnation, proclaimed that Jesus said more about hell than He did about heaven. This is a common misunderstanding of what Jesus taught about hell. Somehow this falsehood got started and is being perpetuated by well-meaning religious leaders who are very badly informed. The Catholic version of this smear of Jesus' Holy name is that He spoke about hell "often."[6]

As I explained in *Spiritual Terrorism*, the truth can be easily ascertained by using a concordance, such as *Strong's Exhaustive Concordance*[7] [based on the KJV which can be Googled at biblestudytools.com and use word search], which lists every word in *the Bible* and the verse in which it occurs. Then simply do a word count. According to Strong's, there are 14 references to hell in the Gospels: eight in Matthew, three in Mark, three in Luke, and zero in John. The rest of the New Testament contains a total of eight references to hell for a total of 22. By no stretch is that a lot, even if you include such verses as Matthew 25:41 and 46 where the word "hell" is not used but after-life accountability is taught.

According to *Strong's*, in regard to the number of times the N. T. writers used the word "heaven" in the Gospels are 74 in Matthew, 17 in Mark, 31 in Luke, and 18 in John for a total of 140. In the rest of the N.T., there are a total of 112 references to heaven for a total of 252 compared to 22 for hell. To get the number of references to hell in perspective is important, but it is even more important to understand what Jesus said and what the N.T. writers wrote and what they meant. To discover the truth, it is crucial to know the KJV indiscriminately translated the Hebrew word "Sheol" and three Greek words: "Hades," "Gehenna," and "Tartarus" as hell. Most modern translations make the distinction in the text or in a footnote. Significantly, those in Gehenna will be "salted with fire," and Hades along with death and the Devil will be cast into "the lake of burning sulfur" (Rev. 20:10-15).

I called the ministry of the radio preacher who proclaimed that Jesus said more about hell than heaven. I got his voice mail, so I left a message that I had heard his radio program, and he had made a factual misstatement about what our Lord Jesus Christ had taught. Since I assumed he would want to know about what he had misspoken, he could return my call. It has been about two years, and I have heard nothing from him, but I have heard him on the radio still preaching that Jesus said more about hell than heaven and that sinners in hell will be tormented forever! It is obvious that some preachers do not want to know the truth, since they are comfortable with what they believe and are making money teaching lies about our loving Lord.

A Trilogy: *The Shack, Love Wins*, and *Spiritual Terrorism*

Fortunately, some Evangelical pastors do want to know the truth. While vacationing in another state, I attended a large, growing Evangelical Church. The pastor preached a very positive message on the resurrection of Christ and God's great love, grace, and mercy which motivated Jesus, God in human form, to come to earth to die so that all sinners might be saved. He concluded his sermon with a plea for unbelievers to get saved before it is forever too late.   He strengthened his plea by including the statement that

203

Jesus said more about hell than heaven. After the service, I waited until the pastor had greeted every one and they had left the church. I then introduced myself, we shook hands, and he invited me to his study where we talked for about an hour.

The Shack

I first complimented him on his positive sermon. When I mentioned his misstatement on how much Jesus spoke about hell, he said that he had always heard that and just assumed it to be true. When he looked it up, he found it not to be true and expressed appreciation for my feedback. His church has a bookstore that sells Christian books. One of the books on display was *The Shack*, by Wm. Paul Young, which has sold over 14 millions of copies.[8] This is a wonderfully enlightening book articulating God's all-encompassing, everlasting, never-failing love.

Young stated in *The Shack* that someday all creation will bow to the Lord of all creation. This obviously is an allusion to Phil. 2:9-11, but, since this is a novel, *The Shack* contains no Biblical references. Some who have read *The Shack* and *Spiritual Terrorism* have said that if you like *The Shack* you will love my book, because it gives the Scripture references to support this same totally loving conception of God. Young and I were in the same Evangelical denomination. I have talked with him, and he told me that he does not endorse books, but he will recommend *Spiritual Terrorism*. I asked this pastor whether he had read *The Shack* and, if so, did he like it and agree with the message. He said that he had read it, and he does agree with the message.

Love Wins

This open-minded pastor also mentioned that he had read Rob Bell's book, *Love Wins*, which presents the possibility that all people may be saved. He said that he hopes Bell is right but is afraid he is wrong. Based on that, I was confident he would like reading, *Spiritual Terrorism*, so I mentioned my book to him. He was interested and said he would get my book and read it ASAP.

We later talked by phone; he had gotten my book, read it, and told me that he really enjoyed reading it and liked the message of CU. He stated that my book is "well researched and well written." He also said that he had never heard of being "salted with fire" and had not known the meaning of brimstone and uses of sulfur. Since he was talking on the insecurity of a cell phone, he did not say whether he now believes in CU, and I did not ask him. If he has come to believe in the validity of CU and word should get out, he might well be condemned as a heretic and fired from his church. He said that we can talk in more detail the next time I visit.

I did visit and he said that those who believe in CU would be welcome in his church. Such open-minded loving pastors do need to be careful of not saying that they personally believe in CU because the religious-thought police are everywhere and always vigilant to combat what they perceive to be the heresy of CU.

If Believing in CU, Speak Softly

Not long after my forced resignation for believing in CU, almost a quarter of a century ago, I visited a large Presbyterian Church in the state of Florida. The pastor was very well educated and preached a powerful message of God's wonderful love and amazing grace. Although he did not come right out and state explicitly that he believed in CU, I was 99 percent confident, based on the content of his sermon, that he was a believer in the truth of CU. After the service I shook hands with him, introduced myself, and asked him if he does believe in universal salvation. He lowered his voice and said, "Yes, but I must not say that too loudly, or some people around here will call me a heretic." So even when pastors believe the truth, they are not free to proclaim it openly without fear of being condemned as a heretic! This is a sad state of affairs in the Christian Church, as a whole, even in the 12th year of the 21st Century! What hope is there for the world?

One open-minded, loving compassionate pastor in an Evangelical denomination has lost three pastorates over preaching "too much love, grace, and mercy of God" after coming to believe in CU. He is now in his fourth pastorate, and he apparently has decided to just believe, not preach CU in order not to risk another termination as he nears retirement.

Other Unlikely Places to Hear the Truth that Frees from Fear

Christian Radio Stations

The public is not likely to get the truth that frees from fear from Christian radio stations. Shortly after *Spiritual Terrorism* was published, I received a call from the host of a Christian radio station. He said that he had heard of my book and wondered if I would be willing to be interviewed about it. I, of course, was very willing to be interviewed in the hope that I would be able to reach more people, especially victims of spiritual abuse, with the Good News of Christian Universalism. This host interviewed me for an hour. When concluded, I asked him how he thought it went. He replied, "Great!" He said that he was looking forward to airing it on his program. I asked him when he thought it would be aired, and he said that he did not know, since he would have to get the approval of his station manager first, but it would probably air in the next couple of days.

He, however, called back a couple of hours later to say that he was sorry, but my interview would not be aired at all, because the manager said that it is too controversial. He was concerned that Christian Churches would think that CU is heresy, and then threaten sponsors with a boycott of their products and services. This could cause advertisers to withdraw their sponsorship. While it is said that controversy can be good for ratings, that is not the case when it comes down to Christian radio stations making a decision about programming which could adversely affect their income from advertising.

Secular Radio Stations

Even secular radio stations and talk show hosts must be on guard against conservative Christian listeners being offended by what is aired on their programs. One talk show host, on a secular station, told me that he liked the all-loving message about God and universal salvation in *Spiritual Terrorism* and would do anything he could to help me spread the Good News. He related that he had been spiritually abused in the Roman Catholic Church as he was growing up and that he is no longer a practicing Catholic. He did interview me a couple of times and said that I was welcome to come back and discuss additional topics in my book. I did contact him about coming back, but I have not heard from him in over two years. I think he must have had some negative feedback with accusations of promoting a particular religious point-of-view.

I have said in every interview that I have done that I am not promoting any particular religion, and I am not saying which is the correct or best religion or denomination. My perspective is that of a public service to help the victims of spiritual abuse/terrorism to understand that there is a more loving conception of God and more positive interpretation of *the Bible* or other holy book of their faith than that to which they have been exposed. This certainly is the case in regard to the spiritual abuse of children. I address the issue of the problem of and the solution to spiritual abuse in all major religions. Victims of spiritual abuse do not need to get a new religion, just a much more loving version of their religion. Neither do they need to become nonreligious to be healed of spiritual abuse. The cure: become spiritual—loving, giving, and forgiving.

A couple of hosts, who interviewed me on a secular radio station, were included in an indictment of me in a letter to the editor of a local newspaper by a Christian Fundamentalist listener who was incensed by what I had said in an interview about legalism and literalism being causes of spiritual abuse. He tacitly threatened the hosts with eternal damnation in hell for even having interviewed me on radio, since I am a heretic. The letter writer stated that I had insulted and assaulted Fundamental Christians (who by definition are literalists, since they proclaim that *the Bible* must be interpreted literally). Even though I am a Trinitarian Christian, his contention was that anyone who believes in CU could not possibly be a true Christian. Of course, according to his belief, the penalty for heresy is eternal punishment in literal hell fire. He is precisely the kind of Christian who needs to hear a totally loving message about God but who is most resistive to it and most adamant about defending the insanely false doctrine of eternal torture in literal hell fire.

Conservative Christian Bookstores

Neither is the public likely to learn the truth that frees from fear from conservative Christian bookstores. I found that such stores would not sell my book, since they considered CU to be heretical. One such store after discovering, through some customers I had referred to that store, the late Christian writer George MacDonald wrote from the perspective of CU decided to stop stocking MacDonald's books. But, since they wanted to make money, they would still order his books if customers asked for them.

An owner of a conservative Christian bookstore, I have known for years, told me that she would not handle my book, since it is "not Biblical" even though she had not and would not read it. When I noticed that the book, *The Shack*, was in the store's display window, I asked, "Are you aware that *The Shack* has the same all-loving conception of God as my book?" She contorted her face and sneered, "I hate *The Shack*" [due to too much of God's love, grace, and mercy]! I said, "Well, nevertheless, you are selling it to make a profit, so why not sell my book?"

She turned away, but the obvious answer is that she wants to believe that she is taking a "principled stand" against a book she perceives to be heretical. She took this stance since it is not a best seller, but she compromised her "principles" on a book with the same message, so her store can make money on that book which had already sold millions of copies. She concluded, "You are so well educated, I can't figure out where you went wrong!" In cordially parting, I asked, "Do you think a good psychological and theological education could be where I went right?"

Here is real irony, in order to get my Christian book into a bookstore and be able to do a book signing it took a secular store whose owner is an atheist! While not agreeing with my theistic perspective, this person said that it is a message of love and peace that the world needs to hear. Oh, that Christians who believe in eternal damnation in hell were that open minded! To be fair and balanced, some Christians who believe in eternal damnation in hell have told me, "I don't know for sure what to believe, but I sure hope that you are right about Christian Universalism!" That reveals their open mindedness and heart of love and compassion.

Sure Place to Find the Truth that Frees from Fear

The best place to find information on the truth that frees from fear is on the Internet—the Information Highway. One can do a word search of such terms as: spiritual abuse/terrorism/insanity, Christian universalism, universal salvation, universal restoration, universal reconciliation, evangelical universalist, scientific universalist, Christian Universalist Association. There are CU blogs on Facebook. Googling my name will reveal a significant amount of information and links to various sites, books, and videos. Googling authors, books, and websites on the resource page and in the bibliography will reveal a wealth of information. Online sellers will not cave in to threats from those opposed to CU.

How the Vast Majority of People Make Decisions

For more than a quarter of a century, I have contended that what people believe about religion has almost nothing to do with religion but almost everything to do with their psychological predisposition. For example, Calvinists are more emotionally comfortable with the certainty of God being sovereign, at the expense of not having free will, while Arminians are more emotionally comfortable with humans having free will, at the expense of God not being sovereign, in regard to salvation.

Some people are emotionally repulsed by the thought of all being saved, since that would include terrible dictators like Hitler. Ditto that for the salvation of mass murderers like Timothy McVeigh and serial murderers like Ted Bundy. But, as I pointed out in *Spiritual Terrorism*, Hitler and McVeigh were Catholics, so unless Christians can lose their salvation, they will be in heaven. McVeigh's last granted request before his execution, for killing 168 people in bombing the Murrah Federal Building, was to have a priest hear his confession. And it was reported by the media that Bundy confessed his sins and accepted Christ as his Savior before his execution by the state of Florida. Some Christians have told me that they have no problem with such felons being saved if they accepted Christ a minute before they died. But they have a terrible emotional problem with good moral people being saved after they die—even those who had never heard the Gospel. Thus, they will not read about CU or even listen to a logical explanation of CU.

To my knowledge there have been no scientific studies demonstrating the role of emotion in decision making in regard to religion. However, Dr. Drew Weston, who is professor of psychology and psychiatry at Emory University, has done scientific studies on decision making in regard to politics. He has written three books and various articles on how people make decisions [Google his name to find more info]. Dr. Weston has shown that people's psychological orientation predicts what decision they will make almost 85 percent of the time!

In essence, when reason says one thing and emotion another, people will make their decisions based on emotion almost every time! This truth can be extrapolated to all areas of life, especially religion. It is like the old saying, "One picture is worth a thousand words." In decision making one emotion is worth a thousand facts! This is the basis of another saying, "Don't confuse me with the facts, my mind is made up."

In this book, I have presented the Biblical and historical facts in regard to the logical truth of CU. But Christians are threatened with eternal torture in hell for not believing in eternal torture! This elicits fear, a powerful emotion, to not consider the truth of CU based on reason. Readers, what decision will you make and on what basis—fear that blinds and binds or love that frees from fear? Since God is love, there is no fear in love. God's love—perfect love—casts out fear (I John 4:8, 18)!

Lessons Learned from My Godly Parents

My Mother and Father were two of the most loving, hard-working, honest persons who ever lived. They taught me by example, as well as words, to always do the right thing regardless of the consequences. For graduation from high school in 1962, they gave me a card with "If," a poem by Rudyard Kipling (1865-1936), printed in it. This poem both expressed their philosophy of life and their desire for the type of man they desired I would become. I knew it meant a lot to them, so it meant a lot to me. I, therefore, memorized all of "If," but, more importantly, I have always done my best to live up to the sentiments expressed in this poem which represented my parents' high aspirations for me. My parents taught me to trust myself even when others would doubt me, and that no one can please every one. They told me Aesop's Fable, "The Man, the Boy, and the Donkey" [can be read online]. The moral of the story is, "To try to please all is to please none." "If," is composed of eight verses with 32 lines [also online]. This is the first verse [so crucial in trusting oneself and standing for truth]:

> If you can keep your head when all about you
> Are losing theirs, and blaming it on you
> If you can trust yourself when all men doubt you,
> But make allowance for their doubting, too...

Former denominational officials twisted my words by saying that I believe even unbelievers will be saved. No, I do not believe that unbelievers will be saved, but I do believe that all unbelievers will become believers. In addition to pastoring an established Evangelical Church for five years, I was the founding pastor of a group of Evangelical believers that grew, in 10 years, from a home Bible study to an average-sized Protestant Church with a beautiful

211

building, in a great location, with planned phases for future growth. But after being forced to resign, by the denominational officials, due to coming to believe in CU [too much love, grace, and mercy], I lost all and had to start ministerial life over again at age 46. Thus, the fourth verse is especially meaningful to me.

> If you can bear to hear the truth you've spoken
> Twisted by knaves to make a trap for fools,
> Or watch the things you gave your life to, broken,
> And stoop and build 'em up with worn-out tools...

Other Christians who had expressed their love for me no longer do so. Some have called me a "heretic." Others will have nothing to do with me. A Christian pastor used me as a sermon illustration of a once-godly pastor who came to believe in universal salvation and lost his own salvation. Others told me that they are praying for me which means that they believe that I will go to hell unless I come to my senses and affirm the doctrine of eternal punishment. Some have expressed hatred for me, since they believe that the doctrine of CU will cause some people to be forever damned to literal hell fire who might otherwise have been saved. The authors of *Evangelical Affirmations* stated that people who believe as I do are teaching doctrine taught by demons and are even doing the work of the Devil! I have forgiven all of those who have slandered me. All of this antagonism and name calling, due to believers motivated by fear-based Christianity, have vividly recalled to mind these lines of "If":

> If being lied about, don't deal in lies,
> Or being hated, don't give way to hating...
> If you can fill the unforgiving minute
> With sixty seconds' worth of distance run,
> Yours is the Earth and everything that's in it,
> And—which is more—you'll be a Man, my Son!

Be a man or woman motivated by love-based Christianity who will study to know the truth and then stand for this truth regardless of the consequences. All those who do will experience the highest commendation of our Lord Jesus Christ who will say on Judgment Day, "Well done, you good and faithful servant...enter into the joy of the Lord" (Mt. 25:21-23). Christian Universalism is the glorious truth that Jesus said would free people from fear. Be spiritually fear free and optimally mentally/emotionally/physically healthy. Believe, live, enjoy, and share it as Christ's ambassadors of peace!

Discussion Questions

1. Had you heard of being "salted with fire"? If so, where?
2. Had you ever heard of the meaning of brimstone and the symbolic use of sulfur? What does it symbolize?

3. Why do you believe there is so little knowledge of Biblical symbolism?
4. Had you heard of Origen and CU? Does CU make sense?

5. Isn't punishing unbaptized infants with eternal banishment from God or "unelect" infants being tormented in hell forever spiritual insanity?
6. If CU is true, what do you think the probability is of most churches today teaching it? Why are so many hostile to it? If in doubt, why not give God the benefit of any doubt?

7. Does the church need another reformation to relearn CU? How can this happen? What can/will you do?

8. Do you believe that you are trusting God for too much or too little? Explain.
9. Did you believe or do you now believe that there will someday be universal confession of faith in Christ, universal salvation, and universal peace? Why or why not?

10. If you believe in CU, are you willing to stand up for this truth regardless of the consequences? What might be some consequences for you? Are you completely free of fear for yourself and loved ones? If not, what prevents you from being totally fear free?

CHRISTIAN UNIVERSALISM (CU) ACTION STEPS

If you liked the spiritually liberating and emotionally healing message in this book, here are a dozen action steps you may choose to take as ambassadors of peace for Christ. This Biblical truth will free victims of spiritual insanity and abuse/terrorism from mental and emotional imprisonment. This truth will also eliminate divisiveness ("us" vs. "them"), bigotry, and hatred and bring peace to our world torn by religious strife. There shall be peace on earth (Isaiah 2:4)!

1. Write a review, with a 5-star rating [if you think it is merited], and post it on Amazon.com with link to my book.
2. Send a copy of CWI to your family and friends.
3. Post it on Facebook with personal recommendation.
4. Start/join a CU blog on FB for peace of mind and world peace.
5. Adopt as your personal theme song, "Let There Be Peace On Earth," and do your part to make it happen.
6. Give a copy of CWI to your pastor and ask him/her to read it and give you his/her opinion.
7. Suggest Sunday school classes—adult and youth—and start a home Bible study on CU with CWI as the format.
8. Share your faith using "Five Liberating Truths" in chapter 8.
9. Do videos of this liberating truth and post on YouTube.
10. Recommend me for local talk radio and TV interviews.
    Contact: dr.boydpurcell@gmail.com
11. Check out a lot of free information on my websites:
    HealingSpiritualTerrorism.com
    ChristianityWithoutInsanity.com
    And forward links to family, friends, and co-workers.
12. For more info see books/websites in resources section.
    Read *Spiritual Terrorism*, study it, and post a review.
    ST reveals universal salvation in all major religions.

As Christ's ambassadors of peace, we can change the world! We can all help fulfill The Great Commission to go into all the world and preach the Gospel (Mt. 28:19, 20), now in the comfort of home via the "miracle" of the Internet.

Recommended Resources on CU

Beauchemin, Gerard. *Hope Beyond Hell: The Righteous Purpose of God's Judgment*. Olmito: Malista Press, 2007 [revised in 2010].

Chevrier, Allan E. *Whatever Became of Melanie?* Hermann: Tentmaker Ministries & Publications, Inc., 2008.*

Evely, Bob. *At the End of the Ages: The Abolition of Hell*. Wilmore: Grace Evangel, 2003.

Ferwerda, Julie. *Raising Hell: Christianity's Most Controversial Doctrine Put Under Fire*. Lander: Vagabond Group, 2011.*

Fristad, Kalen. *Destined For Salvation: God's Promise to Save Everyone*. Kearney: Morris Publishing, 2003 [5th printing 2011].

Linn, Dennis, Matthew, Sheila [Catholics]. *Good Goats: Healing Our Image of God*. Mahwah: Paulist Press, 1994.

MacDonald, George. Michael Phillips (ed). *Knowing the Heart of God*. Minneapolis: Bethany House Publishers, 1990.

Riley, Michael and James William. *Is God Fair? What About Gandhi?* Bloomington: AuthorHouse, 2011.*

Stetson, Eric. *Christian Universalism: God's Good News For All People*. Sparkling Bay: Sparkling Bay Press, 2008.

Talbott, Thomas. *The Inescapable Love of God*. Willamette: Universal Publishers, 1999.

ChristianUniversalist.org, the official website for the Christian Universalist Association; and Tentmaker.org, hosted by Gary Amirault [very comprehensive website].

*CU from perspective of "Ultra-Universalism"

BIBLIOGRAPHY

Introduction

1. Purcell, Boyd. *Spiritual Terrorism: Spiritual Abuse from the Womb to the Tomb*. Bloomington: AuthorHouse, 2008.

Chapter 1

1. Gerstner, John H. *Repent or Perish*. Ligonier: Soli Deo Gloria Publications, 1990.
2. *The Constitution of the Presbyterian Church (U.S.A.): Part I The Book of Confessions.* Louisville: the Office of the General Assembly, 1999.
3. Gerstner. *Repent or Perish*, p.23.
4. Ware, Timothy. *The Orthodox Church.* New York: Penguin Books, 1963. p. 229.

Chapter 2

1. Wiese, Bill. *23 Minutes in Hell.* Lake Mary: Charisma House, 2006.
2. Godsey Kirby. *When We Talk About God...Let's Be Honest.* Macon: Smyth & Helwys Publishing, Inc., 1996.
3. Phillips, Michael R. *George MacDonald: Scotland's Beloved Storyteller,* Minneapolis: Bethany House Pub. 1987.
4. Ibid, p. 14.
5. Linn, Dennis, Matthew, Sheila. *Good Goats: Healing Our Image of God.* Mahwah: Paulist Press, 1994. p. 17.
6. Yalom, Irvin D. *Staring at the Sun: Overcoming the Terror of Death.* San Francisco: Jossey-Bass, 2008.
7. Ibid., p. 5.
8. Ibid., pp. 21; 264.
9. Ibid., p. 22
10. Feifel, Herman, (ed.). *Death and Identity,* "Alexander and Alderstein's Study." New York: McGraw-Hill Book Co., 1959. pp. 272-279.
11. Yalom. *Staring at the Sun.* p. 11.

12. Beauchemin, Gerry. *Hope Beyond Hell*. Olmito: Malista Press, 2007, revised 2010.
13. *Diagnostic and Manuel of Mental Disorders IV*, Washington, DC: American Psychiatric Association.
14. Purcell. *Spiritual Terrorism*. pp. 89-107.

Chapter 3

1. May, Gerald G. *Addiction and Grace: Love and Spirituality in the Healing of Addictions*. San Francisco: HarperCollins Publishers, 1988.
2. Errico, Rocco A. *Let There Be Light*. Smyrna: The Noohra Foundation Publisher, 1994. p. 11.
3. Evans, William B. God's Creative Word. Due West: CE Ministries of Associate Reformed Presbyterian Church, Spring Quarter 2012. p. 9.
4. *Walker, Williston. A History of the Christian Church.* New York: Charles Scribner's Sons, 1949. pp. 15, 16.
5. Cook A. *Alliance Life*, "The Missing Motivation." November 6, 1989.
6. Motlagh H (ed.). *Unto Him Shall We Return.* Wilmette: Baha'i Pub. Trust, 1985.
7. Miller, Bobby. *A Christian Psychiatrist's Prayer: Emotional Healing Through Poetry*. Chesapeake: Christian Psychiatry, Inc., 1992.

Chapter 4

1. Kinnaman, David and Gabe Lyons. *unChristian: What A New Generation Really Thinks About Christianity...And Why It Matters*. Grand Rapids: BakerBooks, 2007.
2. Ibid., p. 14.
3. Ibid., pp. 15-16.
4. Ibid., p. 17.
5. Ibid., p. 18.
6. Ibid., p. 19.
7. Ibid., pp. 25-26.
8. Ibid., pp. 27.
9. Ibid., p. 29.

10. Ibid., p. 33.
11. Ibid., pp. 36, 37
12. Ibid., p. 250.
13. Ibid., p. 249
14. Lyons, Gabe. *THE NEXT CHRISTIANS: The Good News About The End of Christian America—How a New Generation Is Restoring the Faith.* New York: Doubleday, 2010.
15. Ibid., p. 3.
16. Ibid., p. 5.
17. Ibid., p. 19.
18. Ibid., p. 27
19. Ibid., p. 28.
20. Ibid., p. 228.
21. Fox, Matthew. *The Pope's War: Why Ratzinger's Secret Crusade Has Imperiled The Church And How It Can Be Saved.* New York: Sterling Ethos, 2011.
22. LaChance, Albert J. *The Modern Christian Mystic: Finding the Unitive Presence of God.* Berkeley: North Atlantic Books, 2007.
23. *Fox. The Pope's War.* pp. 203-207.

Chapter 5

1. Tasker R.V.G. (ed.). *Tyndale New Testament Commentaries: The Gospel According to St. Matthew.* Grand Rapids: Eerdmans, 1979. p. 240.
2. Errico. *And There Was Light.* p. 9.

Chapter 6

1. Walker. *A History of the Christian Church.* pp. 74-77.
2. Smith G (ed.). *The Tozer Pulpit.* Vol. 8., Harrisburg: Christian Publications, 1981. pp. 24, 25.
3. Baker, Sharon L. *Razing Hell: Rethinking Everything You've Been Told about God's Wrath and Judgment.* Louisville: John Knox Press, 2010. pp. 144, 145.
4. Ferwerda, Julie. *Raising Hell: Christianity's Most Controversial Doctrine Put Under Fire.* Lander: Vagabond, 2011.

5. *Errico. Let There Be Light.* p. 11.
6. Gerstner. *Repent or Perish.* p. 208.
7. Kantzer K (ed.). *Christianity Today*, "Universalism: Will Everyone Be Saved?" March 20, 1987.
8. Warren, Rick. *The Purpose Driven Life.* Grand Rapids: Zondervon, 2002. pp. 22-26.
9. *Walker. A History of the Christian Church.* p. 316.
10. Ibid. pp. 335-357

Chapter 7

1. Errico. *And There Was Light.* p. 98.
2. Ibid. pp. 99-100.
3. Chan, Francis. *Crazy Love.* Colorado Springs: David C. Cook, 2008.
4. Chan, Francis. *Erasing Hell: What God Said about Eternity, and the Things We've Made Up.* Colorado Springs: David C. Cook, 2011. pp. 71-87.
5. Chevrier, Allan E. *Whatever Became of Melanie?* Hermann: Tentmaker Ministries & Publications, Inc., 2nd Ed., 2008.
6. Errico. *And There Was Light.* p. 223.
7. Ibid. p. 225.
8. Ibid. p. 226
9. Purcell. *Spiritual Terrorism.* p. 122.

Chapter 8

1. Hitchens, Christopher. *god is not Great: How Religion Poisons Everything.* New York: Twelve Hachette Book Group, 2007.
2. Russell, Bertrand. *Why I Am Not a Christian.* New York: Simon & Schuster, 1957.
3. Ben-Ami, Jeremy. *A New Voice For Israel: Fighting For The Survival of The Jewish Nation.* Palgrave: MacMillan, 2011.
4. Ibid. p. 160.
5. Ibid. p. 161-162.
6. Ibid. p. 165
7. Ware. *The Orthodox Church.* p. 266.
8. Ibid. p. 267

9. Short, Robert L. *The Parables of Peanuts*. New York: Harper & Row Publishers, 1968. pp. 131-133.
10. Bell, Rob. *Love Wins: A Book About Heaven, and Hell, and the Fate of Every Person Who Ever Lived*. New York: HarperOne. p. 119.
11. Luther, Martin. "Bondage of the Will." pp. 68, 69.
12. Short. *The Parables of Peanuts*. p. 149.

Chapter 9

1. Hawking, Stephen. *A Brief History Of Time*. London: Bantam Books, 1996. pp. 145, 146.
2. Ibid. p. 146.
3. Hawking, Stephen. *The Universe in a Nutshell*. New York: Bantam Books, 2001.
4. Koeing H. et al. (eds.). *Handbook of Religion and Health*. Oxford: Oxford University Press, 2001.
5. Errico. *And There Was Light*. p. 15.
6. Dunn H. *Hard Choices For Loving People.* Herndon: A & A Pub., 2001.
7. Schaeffer, Frank. *Crazy for God: How I Grew up as One of the Elect, Helped Found the Religious Right, and Lived to Take All (or Almost All) of it Back*. Cambridge: Da Capo Press, 2007.

Chapter 10

1. Talbott, Thomas. *The Inescapable Love of God*. Willamette: Universal Publishers, 1999.
2. Ibid. p. 22.
3. Ibid. pp. 218-219.
4. *Bell. Love Wins*.
5. Galli, *Mark. God Wins: Heaven, Hell, and Why the Good New Is Better than Love Wins*. Carol Stream: Tyndale House Publishers, 2011.
6. Ibid., pp. 111, 112.
7. Ibid., p. 112.
8. Tasker. (ed.). 1979. p. 240.

Chapter 11

1. Johnson, Ben Campbell. *Beyond 9/11 Christians & Muslims Together*, Atlanta: The Community Institute Press, 2009.
2. Barclay, Wm. *William Barclay: A Spiritual Autobiography* Grand Rapids: Eerdmans Publishing Co., 1977. pp. 65-67.
3. Chan, Francis and Preston Sprinkle. *Erasing Hell: what God said about eternity and the things we made up.* Colorado Springs: David C. Cook, 2011. pp. 184-186
4. Ibid. p. 186
5. Ibid. pp. 153-155.
6. Moulton, James and George Milligan. *The Vocabulary of The Greek Testament.* Grand Rapids: Eerdmans Pub. Co. 1985. p. 16.
7. Ibid. p. 352.
8. Lyons. *The Next Christians.*
9. Ibid., P. 192
10. Ibid. pp. 192-193
11. Ibid. pp. 193-195.
12. 106. Ibid. p. 198.
13. Ibid. p. 205.

Chapter 12

1. *Good Goats.* Note to the Reader, p. v.
2. Apostolate for Family Consecration: *Catechism of the Catholic Church.* Bloomingdale: John Paul II Holy Family Center, 1994.
3. Ibid.
4. Riley, Michael and James William. *Is God Fair? What About Gandhi?* Bloomington: AuthorHouse, 2011.
5. Evely, Bob. *At the End of the Ages: The Abolition of Hell.* Wilmore: GraceEvangel.org., 2002.
6. Apostolate for Family Consecration: *Catechism of the Catholic Church..*
7. Strong, James. *The Exhaustive Concordance of The Bible.* McLean: MacDonald Publishing Co., pub. date?
8. Young, Wm. Paul. *The Shack: Where Tragedy Confronts Eternity.* Los Angeles: Windblown Media, 2007.

52768162R00122

Made in the USA
Lexington, KY
21 September 2019